Taste of Home
BEST-LOVED
RECIPES

TASTE OF HOME BOOKS • RDA ENTHUSIAST BRANDS, LLC • MILWAUKEE, WI

© 2019 RDA Enthusiast Brands, LLC.
1610 N. 2nd St., Suite 102, Milwaukee WI 53212-3906

Visit us at **tasteofhome.com** for other Taste of Home books and products.

International Standard Book Number:
978-1-61765-825-9
Library of Congress Control Number: 2018963817
Component Number: 118600019H

Deputy Editor: Mark Hagen
Senior Art Director: Raeann Thompson
Editor: Christine Rukavena
Designers: Arielle Jardine, Jazmin Delgado
Copy Editor: Chris McLaughlin

Photographer: Dan Roberts
Senior Set Stylist: Melissa Franco
Food Stylist: Kathryn Conrad

Pictured on front cover:
Slow-Cooker Beef Stew, p. 66
Pictured on title page:
Mom's Italian Bread, p. 194
Pictured on back cover:
Slow-Simmered Meat Ragu, p. 118; Frosted Fudge Brownies, p. 252; Berry-Beet Salad, p. 158
Pictured on spine:
Jumbleberry Crumble, p. 208

Printed in China
1 3 5 7 9 10 8 6 4 2

LIKE US
facebook.com/tasteofhome

TWEET US
twitter.com/tasteofhome

FOLLOW US
@ tasteofhome

PIN US
pinterest.com/taste_of_home

SHOP WITH US shoptasteofhome.com

SHARE A RECIPE tasteofhome.com/submit

12

149

73

46

CONTENTS

AT-A-GLANCE ICONS:

FAST FIX **5 INGREDIENTS**
SLOW COOKER

You'll find dozens of icons
throughout the book. They show
you recipes that are table-ready
in 30 minutes or less,
call for 5 or fewer ingredients,
or use the slow cooker.

FOODS YOU'LL LOVE ALL YEAR

See what online reviewers are saying about our best-loved dishes.
Discover for yourself favorites like...

"Fantastic—I love this sandwich! Feeds a crowd. Best of all, it's one of the rare sandwiches that's not loaded with mayo."
— DAWNLOCKHART

126

"Great BBQ chicken. Slow-baking the chicken first made it juicy and tender. Finished it off on the grill with a North Carolina sauce with the sweet tea. Wonderful Memorial Day dish!"
—CBYBEE

"Great quick dinner with affordable ingredients. Will definitely make again."
—ANGEL182009

102

137

158

"My favorite summertime salad. Makes a great presentation for a luncheon get-together. I serve it with homemade scones. So good!"
—SUEFALK

"The best ham and bean soup I've come across. I look forward to having the ham bone and a little leftover ham from the spiral-cut ham I serve on holidays."
—LIPE.HOUSE

"Mmm...so good! Love the topping. Didn't have enough pecans so mixed them with walnuts. Delicious.
—RECIPEGIRL25

243

62

**APPLE PANCAKES
WITH CIDER SYRUP, 12**

CHAPTER 1

BREAKFAST & BRUNCH

Treat yourself to cinnamon-spiced hotcakes, wholesome baked oatmeal, scrumptious morning sweets and easy overnight casseroles that are perfect for entertaining.

PECAN COFFEE CAKE

My mom serves this nutty coffee cake for Christmas breakfast each year. The simple recipe is a big time-saver on such an event-filled morning. Everyone loves the crunchy topping.
—*Becky Wax, Tuscola, IL*

PREP: 15 min. • **BAKE:** 30 min. • **MAKES:** 15 servings

1 pkg. yellow cake mix (regular size)
1 pkg. (3.4 oz.) instant vanilla pudding mix
1 cup sour cream
4 large eggs
⅓ cup canola oil
2 tsp. vanilla extract
⅔ cup chopped pecans
⅓ cup sugar
2 tsp. ground cinnamon
½ cup confectioners' sugar
2 Tbsp. orange juice

1. In a large bowl, beat the first six ingredients on low speed for 30 seconds. Beat on medium for 2 minutes. Pour into a greased 13x9-in. baking pan. Combine the pecans, sugar and cinnamon; sprinkle over batter. Cut through batter with a knife to swirl pecan mixture.

2. Bake at 350° for 30-35 minutes or until a toothpick inserted in the center comes out clean.

3. Meanwhile, in a small bowl, combine confectioners' sugar and orange juice until smooth; drizzle over warm coffee cake. Cool on a wire rack.

1 PIECE: 335 cal., 16g fat (4g sat. fat), 67mg chol., 332mg sod., 44g carb. (29g sugars, 1g fiber), 4g pro.

CHEESY EGG PUFFS

My father loves to entertain, and these buttery egg delights are a favorite to serve at brunch. The leftovers are perfect to reheat in the microwave on busy mornings, so Dad always stashes a few aside for me to take home once the party is over.
—*Amy Soto, Winfield, KS*

PREP: 15 min. • **BAKE:** 35 min. • **MAKES:** 2½ dozen

½ lb. sliced fresh mushrooms
4 green onions, chopped
1 Tbsp. plus ½ cup butter, cubed, divided
½ cup all-purpose flour
1 tsp. baking powder
½ tsp. salt
10 large eggs, lightly beaten
4 cups shredded Monterey Jack cheese
2 cups 4% cottage cheese

1. In a skillet, saute the mushrooms and onions in 1 Tbsp. butter until tender. In a large bowl, combine the flour, baking powder and salt.

2. In another bowl, combine eggs and cheeses. Melt remaining butter; add to egg mixture. Stir into dry ingredients along with mushroom mixture.

3. Fill greased muffin cups three-fourths full. Bake at 350° for 35-40 minutes or until a knife inserted in the center comes out clean. Carefully run the knife around edge of muffin cups before removing.

2 EGG PUFFS: 275 cal., 21g fat (12g sat. fat), 194mg chol., 486mg sod., 6g carb. (2g sugars, 0 fiber), 16g pro.

✳ READER RAVE

I've made these repeatedly over the years, adding crumbled bacon to them. Many times after baking I will freeze them individually, pull out what I need for breakfast and zap them in the microwave to reheat. They are wonderful and great for low-carb diets!

—BOOTSIEGIRL, TASTEOFHOME.COM

APPLE PANCAKES WITH CIDER SYRUP

Tender pancakes are filled with raisins and minced apple, then drizzled with apple cider syrup. These are wonderful in the summer or on a cool fall morning.
—*April Harmon, Greeneville, TN*

TAKES: 30 min. • **MAKES:** 6 pancakes (⅔ cup syrup)

½   cup all-purpose flour
¼   cup whole wheat flour
2   tsp. sugar
¼   tsp. baking soda
¼   tsp. salt
¼   tsp. ground cinnamon
⅔   cup finely chopped peeled apple
¼   cup raisins
⅔   cup buttermilk
1   large egg, separated
2   tsp. butter, melted
¼   tsp. vanilla extract

SYRUP

¼   cup sugar
2   tsp. cornstarch
⅔   cup apple cider or juice
1   cinnamon stick (1½ in.)
    Dash ground nutmeg
    Additional butter, optional

1. In a small bowl, combine the first six ingredients; stir in apple and raisins. Combine the buttermilk, egg yolk, butter and vanilla; stir into dry ingredients. In a small bowl, beat egg white until soft peaks form; fold into the batter.

2. Pour batter by heaping ¼ cupfuls onto a hot griddle coated with cooking spray; turn when bubbles form on top. Cook until the second side is lightly browned.

3. Meanwhile, in a small saucepan, combine the sugar, cornstarch and cider until smooth; add cinnamon stick. Bring to a boil over medium heat; cook and stir for 2 minutes or until thickened. Discard the cinnamon stick. Stir nutmeg into syrup. Serve the pancakes with warm syrup and, if desired, additional butter.

3 PANCAKES WITH ⅓ CUP SYRUP: 492 cal., 6g fat (3g sat. fat), 116mg chol., 605mg sod., 101g carb. (58g sugars, 4g fiber), 12g pro.

FRUITY BAKED OATMEAL

This is my husband's favorite breakfast treat and the ultimate comfort food. It's warm, filling and always a hit when I serve it to guests.
—*Karen Schroeder, Kankakee, IL*

PREP: 15 min. • **BAKE:** 35 min. • **MAKES:** 9 servings

3 cups quick-cooking oats
1 cup packed brown sugar
2 tsp. baking powder
1 tsp. salt
½ tsp. ground cinnamon
2 large eggs, lightly beaten
1 cup fat-free milk
½ cup butter, melted
¾ cup chopped peeled tart apple
⅓ cup chopped fresh or frozen peaches
⅓ cup fresh or frozen blueberries
Additional fat-free milk, optional

1. Preheat oven to 350°. In a large bowl, combine the oats, brown sugar, baking powder, salt and cinnamon. Combine eggs, milk and butter; add to dry ingredients. Stir in apple, peaches and blueberries.

2. Pour into an 8-in. square baking dish coated with cooking spray. Bake, uncovered, 35-40 minutes or until a knife inserted in center comes out clean. Cut into squares. Serve with milk if desired.

NOTE: If using frozen blueberries, use without thawing to avoid discoloring the batter.

1 PIECE: 322 cal., 13g fat (7g sat. fat), 75mg chol., 492mg sod., 46g carb. (27g sugars, 3g fiber), 7g pro.

BLT EGG BAKE

BLTs are a favorite at my house, so I created this recipe to combine the flavors in a dressier dish. It was such a hit, I served it to my church ladies' group at a brunch. I received lots of compliments and shared the recipe many times that day.
—*Priscilla Detrick, Catoosa, OK*

TAKES: 30 min. • **MAKES:** 4 servings

- ¼ cup mayonnaise
- 5 slices bread, toasted
- 4 slices process American cheese
- 12 bacon strips, cooked and crumbled
- 2 Tbsp. butter
- 2 Tbsp. all-purpose flour
- ¼ tsp. salt
- ⅛ tsp. pepper
- 1 cup 2% milk
- 4 large eggs
- 1 medium tomato, halved and sliced
- ½ cup shredded cheddar cheese
- 2 green onions, thinly sliced
  Shredded lettuce

1. Preheat oven to 325°. Spread mayonnaise on one side of each slice of toast and cut into small pieces. Arrange toast, mayonnaise side up, in a greased 8-in. square baking dish. Top with cheese slices and bacon.

2. In a small saucepan, melt butter. Stir in flour, salt and pepper until smooth. Gradually add the milk and bring to a boil; cook and stir for 2 minutes or until thickened. Pour over bacon.

3. In a large skillet, fry eggs over medium heat until they reach desired doneness; place over bacon. Top with tomato slices; sprinkle with cheddar cheese and onions. Bake, uncovered, 10 minutes. Cut in squares; serve with lettuce.

1 SERVING: 594 cal., 42g fat (16g sat. fat), 251mg chol., 1262mg sod., 25g carb. (7g sugars, 1g fiber), 27g pro.

CINNAMON DOUGHNUT MUFFINS

Back when my children were youngsters, they loved these doughnut muffins as after-school treats or with Sunday brunch.
—*Sharon Pullen, Alvinston, ON*

PREP: 15 min. • **BAKE:** 20 min. • **MAKES:** 10 muffins

1¾ cups all-purpose flour
1½ tsp. baking powder
½ tsp. salt
½ tsp. ground nutmeg
¼ tsp. ground cinnamon
¾ cups sugar
⅓ cup canola oil
1 large egg, lightly beaten
¾ cup whole milk
10 tsp. seedless strawberry or other jam

TOPPING
¼ cup butter, melted
⅓ cup sugar
1 tsp. ground cinnamon

1. In a large bowl, combine flour, baking powder, salt, nutmeg and cinnamon. In a small bowl, combine the sugar, oil, egg and milk; stir into dry ingredients just until moistened.

2. Fill greased or paper-lined muffin cups half full; place 1 tsp. jam on top. Cover jam with enough batter to fill muffin cups three-fourths full. Bake at 350° for 20-25 minutes or until a toothpick comes out clean.

3. Place melted butter in a small bowl; combine sugar and cinnamon in another bowl. Immediately after removing muffins from the oven, dip tops in butter, then in cinnamon sugar. Serve warm.

1 MUFFIN: 288 cal., 13g fat (4g sat. fat), 36mg chol., 240mg sod., 40g carb. (22g sugars, 1g fiber), 4g pro.

BRUNCH HAM ENCHILADAS

When I have company for brunch, this casserole is usually on the menu. With ham, eggs and plenty of cheese, the enchiladas are hearty and fun to eat. And I like that I can make them the day before.

—*Gail Sykora, Menomonee Falls, WI*

PREP: 15 min. + chilling • **BAKE:** 40 min. + standing • **MAKES:** 10 servings

- 2 cups cubed fully cooked ham
- ½ cup chopped green onions
- 10 flour tortillas (8 in.)
- 2 cups shredded cheddar cheese, divided
- 1 Tbsp. all-purpose flour
- 2 cups half-and-half cream
- 6 large eggs, lightly beaten
- ¼ tsp. salt, optional

1. In a large bowl, combine ham and onions; place about ¼ cup down the center of each tortilla. Top with 2 Tbsp. cheese. Roll up and place seam side down in a greased 13x9-in. baking dish.

2. In another large bowl, combine the flour, cream, eggs and, if desired, salt until smooth. Pour over the tortillas. Cover and refrigerate 8 hours or overnight.

3. Remove from the refrigerator 30 minutes before baking. Cover and bake at 350° for 25 minutes. Uncover; bake for 10 minutes. Sprinkle with remaining cheese; bake 3 minutes longer or until the cheese is melted. Let stand for 10 minutes before serving.

1 TORTILLA: 247 cal., 6g fat (4g sat. fat), 28mg chol., 832mg sod., 29g carb. (4g sugars, 1g fiber), 19g pro.

FAMILY-FAVORITE OATMEAL WAFFLES

These healthful waffles are a tried-and-true family favorite—
even with our two children. My husband and I have a small herd
of beef cattle and some pigs. A hearty breakfast really gets us going!
—*Marna Heitz, Farley, IA*

TAKES: 30 min. • **MAKES:** 6 waffles

1½ cups all-purpose flour
 1 cup quick-cooking oats
 3 tsp. baking powder
 ½ tsp. ground cinnamon
 ¼ tsp. salt
 2 large eggs, lightly beaten
1½ cups whole milk
 6 Tbsp. butter, melted
 2 Tbsp. brown sugar
    Assorted fresh fruit and yogurt of your choice

1. In a large bowl, combine flour, oats, baking powder, cinnamon and salt; set aside. In a small bowl, whisk eggs, milk, butter and brown sugar. Add to the flour mixture; stir until blended.

2. Pour batter into a lightly greased waffle maker (amount will vary with size of waffle maker). Close lid quickly. Bake according to manufacturer's directions; do not open during baking. Use fork to remove baked waffle. Top with fresh fruit and yogurt.

1 WAFFLE: 344 cal., 16g fat (9g sat. fat), 99mg chol., 482mg sod., 41g carb. (8g sugars, 2g fiber), 9g pro.

✳ DID YOU KNOW?

Cinnamon comes in two basic types: Ceylon and cassia. Ceylon cinnamon's delicate, complex flavor is ideal for ice creams and simple sauces. The spicy, bolder cassia cinnamon (which is often labeled simply as cinnamon) is preferred for baking.

SAUSAGE & EGG CASSEROLE

For the perfect combination of eggs, sausage, bread and cheese,
this is the dish to try. My mom and I like it because it bakes up tender
and golden, slices beautifully and goes over well whenever we serve it.
—*Gayle Grigg, Phoenix, AZ*

PREP: 15 min. + chilling • **BAKE:** 40 min. • **MAKES:** 10 servings

1 lb. bulk pork sausage
6 large eggs
2 cups milk
1 tsp. salt
1 tsp. ground mustard
6 slices white bread, cut into ½-in. cubes
1 cup shredded cheddar cheese

1. In a skillet, brown and crumble sausage; drain and set aside. In a large bowl, beat eggs; add milk, salt and mustard. Stir in bread cubes, cheese and sausage.

2. Pour into a greased 11x7-in. baking dish. Cover and refrigerate for 8 hours or overnight. Remove from the refrigerator 30 minutes before baking. Bake, uncovered, at 350° for 40 minutes or until a knife inserted in center comes out clean.

1 SERVING: 248 cal., 17g fat (7g sat. fat), 163mg chol., 633mg sod., 11g carb. (4g sugars, 0 fiber), 12g pro.

DOUBLE CHOCOLATE BANANA MUFFINS

Combining two favorite flavors like chocolate and banana makes these rich, soft muffins doubly good.
—*Donna Brockett, Kingfisher, OK*

PREP: 15 min. • **BAKE:** 20 min. • **MAKES:** about 1 dozen

1½ cups all-purpose flour
1 cup sugar
¼ cup baking cocoa
1 tsp. baking soda
½ tsp. salt
¼ tsp. baking powder
1⅓ cups mashed ripe bananas (about 3 medium)
⅓ cup canola oil
1 large egg
1 cup (6 oz.) miniature semisweet chocolate chips

1. Preheat oven to 350°. Whisk together the first six ingredients. In a separate bowl, whisk bananas, oil and egg until blended. Add to flour mixture; stir just until moistened. Fold in chocolate chips.

2. Fill greased or paper-lined muffin cups three-fourths full. Bake until a toothpick inserted in center comes out clean, 20-25 minutes. Cool 5 minutes before removing from pan to a wire rack. Serve warm.

1 MUFFIN (WITHOUT OPTIONAL TOPPING): 278 cal., 11g fat (3g sat. fat), 16mg chol., 220mg sod., 45g carb. (28g sugars, 2g fiber), 3g pro.

OPTIONAL STREUSEL TOPPING: Combine ½ cup sugar, ⅓ cup all-purpose flour and ½ tsp. ground cinnamon; cut in ¼ cup cold butter until crumbly. Before baking, sprinkle over filled muffin cups; bake as directed.

BREAKFAST PIZZA

Pizza for breakfast? Yes, please! I used to make this for my morning drivers when I worked at a pizza delivery place. The quick and easy eye-opener appeals to most.
—*Cathy Shortall, Easton, MD*

....

TAKES: 30 min. • **MAKES:** 8 servings

1 tube (13.8 oz.) refrigerated pizza crust
2 Tbsp. olive oil, divided
6 large eggs
2 Tbsp. water
1 pkg. (3 oz.) bacon bits
1 cup shredded Monterey Jack cheese
1 cup shredded cheddar cheese

1. Preheat oven to 400°. Unroll and press dough onto bottom and ½ in. up sides of a greased 15x10x1-in. pan. Prick thoroughly with a fork; brush with 1 Tbsp. oil. Bake until lightly browned, 7-8 minutes.

2. Meanwhile, whisk together eggs and water. In a nonstick skillet, heat remaining oil over medium heat. Add eggs; cook and stir just until thickened and no liquid egg remains. Spoon over crust. Sprinkle with bacon bits and cheeses.

3. Bake until cheese is melted, 5-7 minutes.

1 PIECE: 352 cal., 20g fat (8g sat. fat), 169mg chol., 842mg sod., 24g carb. (3g sugars, 1g fiber), 20g pro.

✳ TEST KITCHEN TIP

Common olive oil works better for cooking at high heat than virgin or extra-virgin oil. The higher grades have ideal flavor for cold foods, but they smoke at lower temperatures.

SPRINGTIME BEIGNETS & BERRIES

I've always loved beignets, but never thought I could make them myself.
Turns out they're easy! Sometimes I'll even make a quick berry
whipped cream and pipe it inside for a fun surprise.
—*Kathi Hemmer, Grand Junction, CO*

PREP: 25 min. + chilling • **COOK:** 25 min. • **MAKES:** 4 dozen

¼ cup butter, room temperature
¾ cup sugar
½ tsp. salt
½ tsp. ground cinnamon
½ cup plus 2 Tbsp. warm water (120° to 130°), divided
½ cup evaporated milk
1 pkg. (¼ oz.) quick-rise yeast
1 large egg
3¼ to 3¾ cups all-purpose flour
Oil for deep-fat frying
Confectioners' sugar
Berries and whipped topping, optional

1. Beat butter, sugar, salt and cinnamon until crumbly. Beat in ½ cup water and evaporated milk. In another bowl, dissolve yeast in remaining water; add to milk mixture. Beat in egg until blended.

2. Add 2 cups flour; mix until well blended. Stir in enough remaining flour to form a soft dough (dough will be sticky). Place in a greased bowl, turning once to grease the top. Cover; refrigerate 4 hours or overnight.

3. Bring dough to room temperature. On a floured surface, roll dough into a 16x12-in. rectangle. Cut into 2-in. squares. In an electric skillet or deep fryer, heat oil to 375°. Drop beignets, a few at a time, into hot oil. Fry until golden brown, about 1 minute per side. Drain on paper towels. Dust beignets with confectioners' sugar. If desired, serve with berries and whipped topping.

1 BEIGNET: 74 cal., 3g fat (1g sat. fat), 7mg chol., 36mg sod., 10g carb. (3g sugars, trace fiber), 1g pro.

MARMALADE
MEATBALLS, 46

CHAPTER 2

APPETIZERS

Great gatherings call for crowd-pleasing bites by the dozen, and this chapter is packed with fun snacks. Restaurant-style potato skins, nachos and even wontons are surprisingly easy to make at home!

SWEET PEA PESTO CROSTINI

I made a healthier spin on my favorite celebrity chef's recipe by using vegetable broth and going easy on the cheese. The pesto's thick to top crostini. If you want to use it on pasta, add more broth for a sauce-like consistency.
—*Amber Massey, Argyle, TX*

TAKES: 25 min. • **MAKES:** 1½ dozen

12 oz. fresh or frozen peas, thawed
4 garlic cloves, halved
1 tsp. rice vinegar
½ tsp. salt
⅛ tsp. lemon-pepper seasoning
3 Tbsp. olive oil
¼ cup shredded Parmesan cheese
⅓ cup vegetable broth
1 whole wheat French bread demi-baguette (about 6 oz. and 12 in. long)
2 cups cherry tomatoes (about 10 oz.), halved or quartered

1. Preheat broiler. Place the peas, garlic, vinegar, salt and lemon pepper in a blender or food processor; pulse until well blended. Continue processing while gradually adding oil in a steady stream. Add cheese; pulse just until blended. Add broth; pulse until mixture reaches desired consistency.

2. Cut baguette into 20 slices, each ½ in. thick. Place on ungreased baking sheet. Broil 4-5 in. from heat until golden brown, 45-60 seconds per side. Remove to wire rack to cool.

3. To assemble crostini, spread each slice with about 1 Tbsp. pesto mixture; top with tomato pieces.

1 CROSTINI: 77 cal., 2g fat (trace sat. fat), 1mg chol., 190mg sod., 11g carb. (2g sugars, 1g fiber), 3g pro. *Diabetic exchanges:* ½ starch, ½ fat.

BEER DIP

Ranch dressing mix amps up this simple dip. Packed with shredded cheese, it's absolutely perfect with pretzels. The dip can be made with any type of beer, from dark to light and even no-alcohol beer. I've taken it to many parties, where it always disappears and I'm always asked for the recipe.

—*Michelle Long, New Castle, CO*

TAKES: 5 min. • **MAKES:** 3½ cups

2 pkg. (8 oz. each) cream cheese, softened
⅓ cup beer or nonalcoholic beer
1 envelope ranch salad dressing mix
2 cups shredded cheddar cheese
Pretzels

In a large bowl, beat the cream cheese, beer and dressing mix until smooth. Stir in cheddar cheese. Serve with pretzels.

2 TBSP: 89 cal., 8g fat (5g sat. fat), 26mg chol., 177mg sod., 1g carb. (0 sugars, 0 fiber), 3g pro.

✱ READER RAVE

"A friend made this when three of us got together. We used celery, carrot sticks, and green pepper strips— then got out all the crackers and pretzels we could find. Still had some left, so we warmed it a little and spread it on black rye bread with ham. You can't stop eating it once you start!"

—CYNTHIA, TASTEOFHOME.COM

KOREAN WONTONS

Korean wontons (called mandoo) are mild but flavorful, not hot and spicy like many traditional Korean dishes. Filled with inexpensive vegetables and beef, the fried dumplings are very easy to prepare.

—*Christy Lee, Horsham, PA*

PREP: 35 min. • **COOK:** 5 min./batch • **MAKES:** 3 dozen

2 cups shredded cabbage
1 cup canned bean sprouts
½ cup shredded carrots
1½ tsp. plus 2 Tbsp. canola oil, divided
⅓ lb. ground beef
⅓ cup sliced green onions
1½ tsp. sesame seeds, toasted
1½ tsp. minced fresh gingerroot
3 garlic cloves, minced
1½ tsp. sesame oil
½ tsp. salt
½ tsp. pepper
36 wonton wrappers
1 large egg, lightly beaten
3 Tbsp. water

1. In a wok or large skillet, stir-fry the cabbage, bean sprouts and carrots in 1½ tsp. oil until tender; set aside.

2. In a small skillet, cook beef over medium heat until no longer pink; drain. Add to the vegetable mixture. Stir in the onions, sesame seeds, ginger, garlic, sesame oil, salt and pepper.

3. Place about 1 Tbsp. of filling in the center of each wonton wrapper. Combine egg and water. Moisten the wonton edges with egg mixture; fold opposite corners over filling and press to seal.

4. Heat remaining vegetable oil in a large skillet. Cook wontons in batches for 1-2 minutes on each side or until golden brown, adding more oil if needed.

1 WONTON: 94 cal., 4g fat (1g sat. fat), 17mg chol., 172mg sod., 11g carb. (0 sugars, 1g fiber), 4g pro.

PEPPER POPPERS

These creamy stuffed jalapenos have some bite. They may be the most popular treats I make! My husband is always hinting that I should make a batch.
—*Lisa Byington, Johnson City, NY*

PREP: 15 min. • **BAKE:** 25 min. • **MAKES:** about 2 dozen

1 pkg. (8 oz.) cream cheese, softened
1 cup shredded sharp cheddar cheese
1 cup shredded Monterey Jack cheese
6 bacon strips, cooked and crumbled
¼ tsp. salt
¼ tsp. garlic powder
¼ tsp. chili powder
1 lb. fresh jalapenos, halved lengthwise and seeded
½ cup dry bread crumbs
Sour cream, onion dip or ranch salad dressing

1. In a large bowl, combine the cheeses, bacon and seasonings; mix well. Spoon about 2 tablespoonfuls into each pepper half. Roll in bread crumbs.

2. Place in a greased 15x10x1-in. baking pan. Bake, uncovered, at 325° for about15 minutes for spicy flavor, 25 minutes for medium and 35 minutes for mild. Serve with sour cream, dip or dressing.

NOTE: Wear disposable gloves when you are cutting any hot peppers; the oils can burn skin. Avoid touching your face.

1 POPPER: 94 cal., 7g fat (4g sat. fat), 20mg chol., 167mg sod., 4g carb. (1g sugars, 1g fiber), 4g pro.

BLACK BEAN CHICKEN NACHOS

One of my favorite local restaurants, Zeppelins, has the best chicken nachos. Their famous dish inspired me to create my own but with the added convenience of using the slow cooker. I always use fresh cilantro because it's economical and it makes the dish pop with flavor.

—Natalie Hess, Cedar Rapids, IA

PREP: 10 min. • **COOK:** 4 hours • **MAKES:** 8 servings

1½ lbs. boneless skinless chicken breast

2 jars (16 oz. each) black bean and corn salsa

1 each medium green and sweet red pepper, chopped

Tortilla chips

2 cups shredded Mexican cheese blend

Fresh cilantro leaves

Optional toppings: minced fresh cilantro, pickled jalapeno slices and sour cream

1. Place the chicken, salsa and peppers in a 3- or 4-qt. slow cooker. Cook, covered, on low until the meat is tender, 4-5 hours.

2. Remove chicken; shred with two forks. Return to slow cooker. Using a slotted spoon, serve chicken over chips; sprinkle with cheese and cilantro. Add toppings of choice.

½ CUP CHICKEN MIXTURE: 280 cal., 11g fat (5g sat. fat), 72mg chol., 708mg sod., 20g carb. (5g sugars, 8g fiber), 27g pro.

✱ DID YOU KNOW?

If you grow cilantro, you can also harvest its seeds, known as coriander. Let the seeds mature from green to brown, then cut heads with a few inches of stem and hang to dry. Gently loosen the seeds and store in a covered jar.

PARTY SHRIMP

The marinade for this dish makes the shrimp so flavorful, you won't even need a dipping sauce. Even those who claim they don't like shellfish go for this appetizer.
—*Kendra Doss, CO Springs, CO*

PREP: 15 min. + marinating • **BROIL:** 10 min. • **MAKES:** about 2½ dozen

1 Tbsp. olive oil
1½ tsp. brown sugar
1½ tsp. lemon juice
1 garlic clove, thinly sliced
½ tsp. paprika
½ tsp. Italian seasoning
½ tsp. dried basil
¼ tsp. pepper
1 lb. uncooked shrimp (26-30 per lb.), peeled and deveined

1. In a bowl or shallow dish, combine the first eight ingredients. Add the shrimp; toss to coat. Refrigerate for 2 hours.

2. Drain shrimp, discarding marinade. Place shrimp on an ungreased baking sheet. Broil 4 in. from heat until shrimp turn pink, 3-4 minutes on each side.

1 SHRIMP: 14 cal., 0 fat (0 sat. fat), 18mg chol., 18mg sod., 0 carb. (0 sugars, 0 fiber), 2g pro.

✳ TEST KITCHEN TIP

With no-silverware-needed recipes such as this one, tail-on shrimp work best.

MARMALADE MEATBALLS

We had a pre-Super Bowl potluck at work, so I started cooking these meatballs in the morning. By lunchtime they were ready. They were a big hit!
—Jeanne Kiss, Greensburg, PA

PREP: 10 min. • **COOK:** 4 hours • **MAKES:** about 5 dozen

1 bottle (16 oz.) Catalina salad dressing
1 cup orange marmalade
3 Tbsp. Worcestershire sauce
½ tsp. crushed red pepper flakes
1 pkg. (32 oz.) frozen fully cooked home-style meatballs, thawed

In a 3-qt. slow cooker, combine the salad dressing, marmalade, Worcestershire sauce and pepper flakes. Stir in meatballs. Cover and cook on low for 4-5 hours or until heated through.

FREEZE OPTION: Freeze cooled meatball mixture in freezer containers. To use, partially thaw in refrigerator overnight. Microwave, covered, on high in a microwave-safe dish until heated through, gently stirring and adding a little water if necessary.

1 MEATBALL: 73 cal., 4g fat (1g sat. fat), 12mg chol., 126mg sod., 6g carb. (5g sugars, 0 fiber), 2g pro.

EASY PARTY MEATBALLS: Omit first four ingredients. Combine 1 bottle (14 oz.) ketchup, ¼ cup A.1. steak sauce, 1 Tbsp. minced garlic and 1 tsp. Dijon mustard in slow cooker; stir in meatballs. Cook as directed.

SAVORY POTATO SKINS

For a simple snack that really hits the spot on a cool fall
evening, put together a plate of these crisp potato skins.
—*Andrea Holcomb, Torrington, CT*

PREP: 1¼ hours • **BROIL:** 5 min. • **MAKES:** 32 appetizers

4 **large baking potatoes
   (about 12 oz. each)**
3 **Tbsp. butter, melted**
1 **tsp. salt**
1 **tsp. garlic powder**
1 **tsp. paprika**
   **Sour cream and chives,
   optional**

1. Preheat oven to 375°. Scrub the potatoes; pierce several times with a fork. Place on a greased baking sheet; bake until tender, 1 to 1¼ hours. Cool slightly.

2. Cut each potato lengthwise in half. Scoop out pulp, leaving ¼-in. thick shells (save pulp for another use).

3. Cut each half shell lengthwise into quarters; return to baking sheet. Brush insides with butter. Mix the seasonings; sprinkle over butter.

4. Broil potato wedges 4-5 in. from heat until golden brown, 5-8 minutes. If desired, mix sour cream and chives and serve with potato skins.

1 WEDGE: 56 cal., 2g fat (1g sat. fat), 6mg chol., 168mg sod., 8g carb. (0 sugars, 1g fiber), 1g pro.

MEDITERRANEAN TOMATO BITES

My friend Mary served these lovely appetizers at a gathering several years ago, and I adapted it a bit to my taste. It's a great summertime recipe when tomatoes and herbs are at their freshest.

—*Susan Wilson, Milwaukee, WI*

PREP: 20 min. • **BAKE:** 15 min. • **MAKES:** 32 appetizers

1 pkg. (17.3 oz.) frozen puff pastry, thawed
1½ cups shredded Gouda cheese
6 plum tomatoes, thinly sliced
¼ cup pitted ripe olives, coarsely chopped
1 cup crumbled feta cheese
Minced fresh basil
Minced fresh oregano

1. Preheat oven to 400°. Unfold puff pastry. Cut each sheet into 16 squares; place on parchment paper-lined baking sheets.

2. Sprinkle with Gouda cheese; top with tomatoes, olives and feta cheese. Bake until golden brown, 14-18 minutes. Sprinkle with herbs.

FREEZE OPTION: Cover and freeze unbaked pastries on waxed paper-lined baking sheets until firm. Transfer to freezer containers, separating layers with waxed paper; return to freezer. To use, bake the pastries as directed, increasing time as necessary to heat through. Sprinkle with herbs.

1 APPETIZER: 106 cal., 6g fat (2g sat. fat), 8mg chol., 136mg sod., 9g carb. (0 sugars, 1g fiber), 3g pro.

❋ TEST KITCHEN TIP

Puff pastry is convenient, but it's very rich. Lighten up this appetizer by serving on toasted French bread slices instead. Decrease the bake time slightly and skip the Freeze Option.

SESAME CHICKEN BITES

These bites have been a party favorite at our house for many years.
You can make the sauce the night before to make the prep even easier.
—*Kathy Green, Layton, NJ*

....

TAKES: 30 min. • **MAKES:** about 2½ dozen (¾ cup sauce)

SAUCE
- ¾ cup mayonnaise
- 4 tsp. honey
- 1½ tsp. Dijon mustard

CHICKEN
- ½ cup dry bread crumbs
- ¼ cup sesame seeds
- 2 tsp. minced fresh parsley
- ½ cup mayonnaise
- 1 tsp. onion powder
- 1 tsp. ground mustard
- ¼ tsp. pepper
- 1 lb. boneless skinless chicken breasts, cut into 1-in. cubes
- 2 to 4 Tbsp. canola oil

1. In a small bowl, mix sauce ingredients. Refrigerate until serving.

2. In a shallow bowl, mix the bread crumbs, sesame seeds and parsley. In a separate shallow bowl, mix mayonnaise and seasonings. Dip the chicken cubes in the mayonnaise mixture, then in crumb mixture, patting to help coating adhere to all sides.

3. In a large skillet, heat 2 Tbsp. of oil over medium-high heat. Add chicken in batches; cook until chicken is no longer pink, turning occasionally and adding additional oil as needed. Serve with sauce.

1 CHICKEN BITE WITH ABOUT 1 TSP. SAUCE: 102 cal., 9g fat (1g sat. fat), 9mg chol., 73mg sod., 2g carb. (1g sugars, 0 fiber), 4g pro.

CHEDDAR-VEGGIE APPETIZER TORTE

A line forms quickly behind this quiche-like torte at family gatherings.
The wedges are easy to eat as finger food, and it's delicious hot or cold.

—Barb Estabrook, Appleton, WI

PREP: 25 min. • **BAKE:** 30 min. + cooling • **MAKES:** 16 servings

1⅓ cups finely crushed multigrain crackers

¼ cup butter, melted

2 cups shredded sharp cheddar cheese

1 small zucchini, finely chopped

½ cup sliced fresh mushrooms

⅓ cup finely chopped red onion

¼ cup finely chopped sweet red pepper

1 Tbsp. olive oil

1 carton (8 oz.) spreadable garlic and herb cream cheese

4 large eggs, lightly beaten

2 Tbsp. crumbled cooked bacon

2 Tbsp. grated Parmesan cheese

1. In a small bowl, combine cracker crumbs and butter. Press onto the bottom of a greased 9-in. springform pan. Sprinkle with cheddar cheese. In a large skillet, saute the zucchini, mushrooms, onion and red pepper in oil until tender. Spoon over cheese.

2. In a large bowl, beat cream cheese until smooth. Add eggs; beat on low speed just until combined. Stir in bacon. Pour over vegetable mixture. Sprinkle with Parmesan cheese.

3. Place pan on a baking sheet. Bake torte at 375° for 30-35 minutes or until center is almost set. Cool on a wire rack for 10 minutes. Carefully run a knife around edge of pan to loosen; remove sides of pan. Serve warm or chilled. Refrigerate leftovers.

1 SLICE: 175 cal., 15g fat (8g sat. fat), 81mg chol., 244mg sod., 3g carb. (1g sugars, 0 fiber), 6g pro.

FRESH FROM THE GARDEN WRAPS

We moved into a house with a garden that needed tending. Using the herbs we found, we made these fresh-tastic wraps for our first dinner there.
—*Chris Bugher, Asheville, NC*

PREP: 20 min. + standing • **MAKES:** 8 servings

1 medium ear sweet corn
1 medium cucumber, chopped
1 cup shredded cabbage
1 medium tomato, chopped
1 small red onion, chopped
1 jalapeno pepper, seeded and minced
1 Tbsp. minced fresh basil
1 Tbsp. minced fresh cilantro
1 Tbsp. minced fresh mint
⅓ cup Thai chili sauce
3 Tbsp. rice vinegar
2 tsp. reduced-sodium soy sauce
2 tsp. creamy peanut butter
8 Bibb or Boston lettuce leaves

1. Cut corn from cob and place in a large bowl. Add cucumber, cabbage, tomato, onion, jalapeno and herbs.

2. Whisk together chili sauce, vinegar, soy sauce and peanut butter. Pour over vegetable mixture; toss to coat. Let stand 20 minutes.

3. Using a slotted spoon, place ½ cup salad in each lettuce leaf. Fold lettuce over filling.

NOTE: Wear disposable gloves when you are cutting any hot peppers; the oils can burn skin. Avoid touching your face.

1 LETTUCE WRAP: 64 cal., 1g fat (0 sat. fat), 0 chol., 319mg sod., 13g carb. (10g sugars, 2g fiber), 2g pro. *Diabetic exchanges:* 1 vegetable, ½ starch.

AUSSIE SAUSAGE ROLLS

I was born and raised in Australia but moved to the U.S. when I married my husband. When I long for a taste of my homeland, I bake up a batch of these cute little sausage rolls and share them with my neighbors or co-workers.
—*Melissa Landon, Port Charlotte, FL*

PREP: 30 min. • **BAKE:** 20 min. • **MAKES:** 3 dozen

1 medium onion, finely chopped
2 Tbsp. minced fresh chives or 2 tsp. dried chives
2 tsp. minced fresh basil or ½ tsp. dried basil
2 garlic cloves, minced
½ tsp. salt
¼ tsp. pepper
1 tsp. paprika, divided
1¼ lbs. bulk pork sausage
1 pkg. (17.3 oz.) frozen puff pastry, thawed

1. Preheat oven to 350°. Combine the onion, chives, basil, garlic, salt, pepper and ¾ tsp. paprika. Add the sausage; mix lightly but thoroughly.

2. On a lightly floured surface, roll each pastry sheet into an 11x10½-in. rectangle. Cut lengthwise into three strips. Spread ½ cup sausage mixture lengthwise down the center of each strip. Fold over sides, pinching edges to seal. Cut each log into six pieces.

3. Place on a rack in a 15x10x1-in. pan, seam side down. Sprinkle with remaining paprika. Bake until the rolls are golden brown and sausage is no longer pink, 20-25 minutes.

1 APPETIZER: 116 cal., 8g fat (2g sat. fat), 11mg chol., 198mg sod., 8g carb. (0 sugars, 1g fiber), 3g pro.

**QUICK CHICKEN
& DUMPLINGS, 78**

CHAPTER 3

SOUPS, STEWS & CHILI

Nothing warms the heart like a steaming bowlful of homemade soup. Need some comfort food to take off the chill or to share with your neighbors and friends? Look here for our readers' top picks.

NEIGHBORHOOD BEAN SOUP

Even though I'm single, I make multiple servings of everything. Actually, this tendency has helped me to get to know my neighbors. A few of them always volunteer to be my guinea pigs when I try out a new recipe or two.
—*Cheryl Trowbridge, Windsor, ON*

. . . .

PREP: 30 min. + standing • **COOK:** 2¼ hours • **MAKES:** 10 servings (2½ qt.)

2 cups dried great northern beans
5 cups chicken broth
3 cups water
1 meaty ham bone or 2 smoked ham hocks
2 to 3 Tbsp. chicken bouillon granules
1 tsp. dried thyme
½ tsp. dried marjoram
½ tsp. pepper
¼ tsp. rubbed sage
¼ tsp. dried savory
2 medium onions, chopped
3 medium carrots, chopped
3 celery ribs, chopped
1 Tbsp. canola oil

1. Sort beans and rinse with cold water. Place beans in a Dutch oven; add water to cover by 2 in. Bring to a boil; boil for 2 minutes. Remove from the heat; cover and let soak for 1-4 hours or until beans are softened.

2. Drain and rinse beans, discarding liquid. Return beans to pan; add broth, 3 cups water, ham bone, bouillon and seasonings; bring to a boil. Reduce the heat; cover and simmer for 1½ hours.

3. Meanwhile, in a large skillet, saute the onions, carrots and celery in oil until tender; add to soup. Cover and simmer soup 45-60 minutes longer or until beans are tender.

4. Remove ham bone; cool slightly. Skim fat from soup. Remove meat from bone and cut into chunks; return to soup. Discard bone.

1 CUP: 203 cal., 5g fat (1g sat. fat), 11mg chol., 1001mg sod., 29g carb. (6g sugars, 9g fiber), 13g pro.

CHEDDAR POTATO CHOWDER

I made this soup only occasionally because the original recipe was quite high in fat. I doctored it up a bit, using healthier ingredients, and now we eat this rich, flavorful chowder more often.

—*Ellie Rausch, Goodsoil, SK*

PREP: 20 min. • **COOK:** 20 min. • **MAKES:** 7 servings

2 cups water
2 cups diced unpeeled red potatoes
1 cup diced carrot
½ cup diced celery
¼ cup chopped onion
1 tsp. salt
¼ tsp. pepper
¼ cup all-purpose flour
2 cups 2% milk
2 cups shredded reduced-fat cheddar cheese
1 cup cubed fully cooked ham

1. In a Dutch oven, combine the first seven ingredients. Bring to a boil. Reduce the heat; cover and simmer for 10-12 minutes or until tender.

2. Meanwhile, place the flour in a large saucepan; gradually whisk in milk. Bring to a boil over medium heat; cook and stir for 2 minutes or until thickened. Remove from the heat. Add cheese; stir until melted. Stir the ham and the cheese sauce into undrained vegetables; stir until combined.

1 CUP: 212 cal., 9g fat (5g sat. fat), 29mg chol., 847mg sod., 18g carb. (0 sugars, 2g fiber), 16g pro.

SLOW-COOKER BEEF STEW

When there's a chill in the air, I love to make my slow-cooked stew.
It's chock-full of tender chunks of beef, potatoes and carrots.
—*Earnestine Wilson, Waco, TX*

PREP: 25 min. • **COOK:** 8½ hours • **MAKES:** 8 servings (2 qt.)

1½ lbs. potatoes, peeled and cubed

6 medium carrots, cut into 1-in. lengths

1 medium onion, coarsely chopped

3 celery ribs, coarsely chopped

3 Tbsp. all-purpose flour

1½ lbs. beef stew meat, cut into 1-in. cubes

3 Tbsp. canola oil

1 can (14½ oz.) diced tomatoes, undrained

½ to 1 cup beef broth

1 tsp. ground mustard

½ tsp. salt

½ tsp. pepper

½ tsp. dried thyme

½ tsp. browning sauce, optional

1. Layer the potatoes, carrots, onion and celery in a 5-qt. slow cooker. Place flour in a large resealable plastic bag. Add stew meat; seal and toss to coat evenly. In a large skillet, brown meat in oil in batches. Place over vegetables.

2. In a large bowl, combine the tomatoes, broth, mustard, salt, pepper, thyme and, if desired, browning sauce. Pour over the beef. Cover and cook on high for 1½ hours. Reduce heat to low; cook 7-8 hours longer or until meat and vegetables are tender.

1 CUP: 272 cal., 11g fat (3g sat. fat), 53mg chol., 381mg sod., 23g carb. (7g sugars, 4g fiber), 19g pro.

✱ TEST KITCHEN TIP

Give limp celery a second chance to season entrees, soups and stews. Cut the ends from the limp celery stalks and place the stalks in a glass of cold water in the refrigerator for several hours or overnight. You'll be surprised how refreshed the celery will be.

RED PEPPER SOUP

While I don't have scientific proof of it, Red Pepper Soup works for me as
a head cold remedy! It's a good gift to take when visiting a sick friend, too.
For a pretty touch, top the soup with grated cheese and parsley. We enjoy it
with jalapeno cheese buns. You can also serve it with warm garlic bread.
—*Barb Nelson, Victoria, BC*

PREP: 35 min. • **COOK:** 20 min. + cooling • **MAKES:** 12 servings (about 3 qt.)

6 medium sweet red peppers, chopped
2 medium carrots, chopped
2 medium onions, chopped
1 celery rib, chopped
4 garlic cloves, minced
1 Tbsp. olive oil
2 cans (one 49½ oz., one 14½ oz.) chicken broth
½ cup uncooked long grain rice
2 Tbsp. minced fresh thyme or 2 tsp. dried thyme
1½ tsp. salt
¼ tsp. pepper
⅛ to ¼ tsp. cayenne pepper
⅛ to ¼ tsp. crushed red pepper flakes

1. In a Dutch oven, saute red peppers, carrots, onions, celery and garlic in oil until tender.

2. Stir in the chicken broth, rice, thyme, salt, pepper and cayenne; bring to a boil. Reduce heat; cover and simmer for 20-25 minutes or until vegetables and rice are tender.

3. Cool for 30 minutes. Puree in small batches in a blender; return to pan. Add red pepper flakes; heat soup through.

1 CUP: 83 cal., 2g fat (0 sat. fat), 3mg chol., 962mg sod., 14g carb. (4g sugars, 2g fiber), 2g pro.

MEXICAN CHICKEN CORN CHOWDER

I like to make this creamy soup when company
comes to visit. Its zippy flavor is full of southwestern flair.
Sometimes I top it with toasted strips of cut-up leftover tortillas.
—*Susan Garoutte, Georgetown, TX*

TAKES: 30 min. • **MAKES:** 8 servings (2 qt.)

1½ lbs. boneless skinless chicken breasts, cut into 1-in. pieces
½ cup chopped onion
3 Tbsp. butter
1 to 2 garlic cloves, minced
1 cup hot water
2 tsp. chicken bouillon granules
½ to 1 tsp. ground cumin
2 cups half-and-half cream
2 cups shredded Monterey Jack cheese
1 can (14¾ oz.) cream-style corn
1 can (4 oz.) chopped green chilies, undrained
¼ to 1 tsp. hot pepper sauce
1 medium tomato, chopped
 Minced fresh cilantro, fried tortilla strips, optional

1. In a Dutch oven, brown the chicken and onion in butter until chicken is no longer pink. Add garlic; cook 1 minute longer. Add the water, bouillon and cumin; bring to a boil. Reduce heat; cover and simmer for 5 minutes.

2. Stir in cream, cheese, corn, chilies and hot pepper sauce. Cook and stir over low heat until the cheese is melted; add tomato. If desired, top with cilantro and tortilla strips.

1 CUP: 368 cal., 21g fat (13g sat. fat), 114mg chol., 753mg sod., 14g carb. (5g sugars, 1g fiber), 28g pro.

SLOW-COOKER SPICY PORK CHILI

Tender pork adds extra heartiness to this slow-cooked chili. You can use pork tenderloin, boneless pork roast or boneless pork chops for the pork the recipe calls for.
—Taste of Home *Test Kitchen*

PREP: 10 min. • **COOK:** 6 hours • **MAKES:** 6 servings

2 lbs. boneless pork, cut into ½-in. cubes
1 Tbsp. canola oil
1 can (28 oz.) crushed tomatoes
2 cups frozen corn
1 can (15 oz.) black beans, rinsed and drained
1 cup chopped onion
2 cups beef broth
1 can (4 oz.) chopped green chilies
1 Tbsp. chili powder
1 tsp. minced garlic
½ tsp. salt
½ tsp. cayenne pepper
½ tsp. pepper
¼ cup minced fresh cilantro
Shredded cheddar cheese, optional

1. In a large skillet, cook pork in oil over medium-high heat for 5-6 minutes or until browned. Transfer pork and drippings to a 5-qt. slow cooker. Stir in tomatoes, corn, beans, onion, broth, chilies, chili powder, garlic, salt, cayenne and pepper.

2. Cover and cook on low for 6-7 hours or until pork is tender. Stir in cilantro. Serve with cheese if desired.

1¾ CUPS: 395 cal., 12g fat (4g sat. fat), 89mg chol., 1055mg sod., 34g carb. (9g sugars, 8g fiber), 39g pro.

COMFORTING CHICKEN NOODLE SOUP

A good friend made us this rich, comforting soup after the birth of our son. It was such a help to have dinner taken care of until I was back on my feet. Now I give a pot of this yummy soup (along with the recipe) to other new mothers.
—*Joanna Sargent, Sandy, UT*

TAKES: 25 min. • **MAKES:** 12 servings (about 3 qt.)

2 qt. water
8 tsp. chicken bouillon granules
6½ cups uncooked wide egg noodles
2 cans (10¾ oz. each) condensed cream of chicken soup, undiluted
3 cups cubed cooked chicken
1 cup sour cream
Minced fresh parsley

1. In a large saucepan, bring water and bouillon to a boil. Add noodles; cook, uncovered, until tender, about 10 minutes. Do not drain. Add soup and chicken; heat mixture through.

2. Remove from the heat; stir in the sour cream. Sprinkle with minced parsley.

1 CUP: 218 cal., 9g fat (4g sat. fat), 67mg chol., 980mg sod., 18g carb. (2g sugars, 1g fiber), 15g pro.

LENTIL & CHICKEN SAUSAGE STEW

This hearty and healthy stew will warm your family right down to their toes! Serve with cornbread or rolls to soak up every last morsel.
—*Jan Valdez, Chicago, IL*

PREP: 15 min. • **COOK:** 8 hours • **MAKES:** 6 servings

1 carton (32 oz.) reduced-sodium chicken broth

1 can (28 oz.) diced tomatoes, undrained

3 fully cooked spicy chicken sausage links (3 oz. each), cut into ½-in. slices

1 cup dried lentils, rinsed

1 medium onion, chopped

1 medium carrot, chopped

1 celery rib, chopped

2 garlic cloves, minced

½ tsp. dried thyme

In a 4- or 5-qt. slow cooker, combine all ingredients. Cover and cook on low for 8-10 hours or until lentils are tender.

1½ CUPS: 231 cal., 4g fat (1g sat. fat), 33mg chol., 803mg sod., 31g carb. (8g sugars, 13g fiber), 19g pro. *Diabetic exchanges:* 2 lean meat, 2 vegetable, 1 starch.

✳ DID YOU KNOW?

Ounce for ounce, lentils have as much protein as steak (with less than 10 percent of the fat!). A half-cup of cooked lentils provides you with nine grams of protein and eight grams of healthy fiber—that's almost a third of the daily recommended amount.

QUICK CHICKEN & DUMPLINGS

Oh, the things you can make with frozen biscuit dough. I like
to use buttermilk biscuits to make this easy dumpling dish.
—*Lakeya Astwood, Schenectady, NY*

....

TAKES: 30 min. • **MAKES:** 6 servings

- 6 **individually frozen biscuits**
- ¼ **cup chopped onion**
- ¼ **cup chopped green pepper**
- 1 **Tbsp. olive oil**
- 4 **cups shredded rotisserie chicken**
- 3 **cans (14½ oz. each) reduced-sodium chicken broth**
- 1 **can (4 oz.) mushroom stems and pieces, drained**
- 1 **tsp. chicken bouillon granules**
- 1 **tsp. minced fresh parsley**
- ½ **tsp. dried sage leaves**
- ¼ **tsp. dried rosemary, crushed**
- ¼ **tsp. pepper**

1. Cut each biscuit into fourths; set aside. In a large saucepan, saute onion and green pepper in oil until tender. Stir in the chicken, broth, mushrooms, bouillon granules, parsley, sage, rosemary and pepper.

2. Bring to a boil. Reduce heat; add the biscuits for dumplings. Cover and simmer for 10 minutes or until a toothpick inserted in the center of a dumpling comes out clean (do not lift cover while simmering).

1½ CUPS: 420 cal., 20g fat (5g sat. fat), 83mg chol., 1443mg sod., 26g carb. (6g sugars, 1g fiber), 34g pro.

TUSCAN PORK STEW

Tender chunks of pork slowly cook in a nicely seasoned, wine-infused sauce. Add some crushed red pepper flakes for a little added kick.
—*Penny Hawkins, Mebane, NC*

PREP: 15 min. • **COOK:** 8½ hours • **MAKES:** 8 servings (2 qt.)

1½ lbs. boneless pork loin roast, cut into 1-in. cubes

2 Tbsp. olive oil

2 cans (14½ oz. each) Italian diced tomatoes, undrained

2 cups reduced-sodium chicken broth

2 cups frozen pepper stir-fry vegetable blend, thawed

½ cup dry red wine or additional reduced-sodium chicken broth

¼ cup orange marmalade

2 garlic cloves, minced

1 tsp. dried oregano

½ tsp. fennel seed

½ tsp. pepper

⅛ tsp. crushed red pepper flakes, optional

2 Tbsp. cornstarch

2 Tbsp. cold water

Hot cooked fettuccine, optional

1. In a large skillet, brown pork in oil; drain. Transfer to a 5-qt. slow cooker.

2. Stir in the tomatoes, broth, vegetable blend, wine, marmalade, garlic, oregano, fennel seed, pepper and pepper flakes if desired. Cover and cook on low for 8-10 hours or until meat is tender.

3. Combine the cornstarch and water until smooth; gradually stir into stew. Cover and cook on high for 30 minutes or until thickened. Serve with fettuccine if desired.

1 CUP: 232 cal., 7g fat (2g sat. fat), 42mg chol., 614mg sod., 19g carb. (12g sugars, 1g fiber), 19g pro. *Diabetic exchanges:* 2 lean meat, 1 starch, 1 vegetable, ½ fat.

SPICED-UP HEALTHY SOUP

This has been a hit with our family and friends. It's spicy,
low-fat and filled with good-for-you ingredients.
—*Diane Tayman, Dixon, IL*

PREP: 15 min. • **COOK:** 40 min. • **MAKES:** 14 servings (3½ qt.)

1   medium onion,
    chopped
⅓   cup medium pearl
    barley
2   Tbsp. canola oil
4   garlic cloves, minced
5   cans (14½ oz. each)
    reduced-sodium chicken
    broth
2   boneless skinless
    chicken breast halves
    (4 oz. each)
1   cup dried lentils, rinsed
1   jar (16 oz.) picante sauce
1   can (15 oz.) garbanzo
    beans or chickpeas,
    rinsed and drained
½   cup minced fresh
    cilantro
8   cups chopped fresh
    spinach

1. In a Dutch oven, saute onion and barley in oil until onion is tender. Add garlic; cook 1 minute longer. Add the broth, chicken and lentils; bring to a boil. Reduce heat; cover and simmer for 15 minutes or until chicken is no longer pink. Remove chicken and set aside.

2. Add the picante sauce, garbanzo beans and cilantro to soup; cover and simmer 10 minutes longer or until barley and lentils are tender.

3. Shred the chicken with two forks. Add spinach and chicken to soup. Simmer, uncovered, for 5 minutes or until spinach is wilted.

1 CUP: 156 cal., 3g fat (0 sat. fat), 9mg chol., 601mg sod., 21g carb. (4g sugars, 7g fiber), 11g pro. *Diabetic exchanges:* 1 starch, 1 lean meat, 1 vegetable, ½ fat.

ASIAN VEGETABLE-BEEF SOUP

My husband is Korean-American, and I enjoy working Asian flavors into our menu. This tasty soup was something I put together one night with what I found in our fridge. Everyone loved it!

—*Mollie Lee, Rockwall, TX*

PREP: 30 min. • **COOK:** 1¾ hours • **MAKES:** 6 servings

1 lb. beef stew meat, cut into 1-in. cubes
1 Tbsp. canola oil
2 cups water
1 cup beef broth
¼ cup sherry or additional beef broth
¼ cup reduced-sodium soy sauce
6 green onions, chopped
3 Tbsp. brown sugar
2 garlic cloves, minced
1 Tbsp. minced fresh gingerroot
2 tsp. sesame oil
¼ tsp. cayenne pepper
1½ cups sliced fresh mushrooms
1½ cups julienned carrots
1 cup sliced bok choy
1½ cups uncooked long grain rice
   Chive blossoms, optional

1. In a large saucepan, brown meat in oil on all sides; drain. Add the water, broth, sherry, soy sauce, onions, brown sugar, garlic, ginger, sesame oil and cayenne. Bring to a boil. Reduce the heat; cover and simmer for 1 hour.

2. Stir in the mushrooms, carrots and bok choy; cover and simmer 20-30 minutes longer or until vegetables are tender. Meanwhile, cook the rice according to package directions.

3. Divide rice among six soup bowls, ¾ cup in each; top each with 1 cup of soup. Garnish soup with chive blossoms if desired.

1 CUP SOUP WITH ¾ CUP RICE: 379 cal., 10g fat (2g sat. fat), 47mg chol., 621mg sod., 50g carb. (9g sugars, 2g fiber), 20g pro.

SPICY SEAFOOD STEW

The hardest part of this quick and easy recipe is peeling and dicing the potatoes—and you can even do that the night before. Just place the potatoes in water and store them in the refrigerator overnight to speed up assembly the next day.

—Bonnie Marlow, Ottoville, OH

PREP: 30 min. • **COOK:** 4¾ hours • **MAKES:** 9 servings (about 2 qt.)

2   lbs. potatoes, peeled and diced
1   lb. carrots, sliced
1   jar (24 oz.) pasta sauce
2   jars (6 oz. each) sliced mushrooms, drained
1½ tsp. ground turmeric
1½ tsp. minced garlic
1   tsp. cayenne pepper
¼   tsp. salt
1½ cups water
1   lb. sea scallops
1   lb. uncooked shrimp (31-40 per lb.), peeled and deveined

In a 5-qt. slow cooker, combine the first eight ingredients. Cook, covered, on low until potatoes are tender, 4½ to 5 hours. Stir in water, scallops and shrimp. Cook, covered, until the scallops are opaque and shrimp turn pink, 15-20 minutes longer.

1 CUP: 229 cal., 2g fat (0 sat. fat), 73mg chol., 803mg sod., 34g carb. (10g sugars, 6g fiber), 19g pro.

✳ READER RAVE

"I made this recipe not once, but twice—and I see a third time in the near future."

—ARITCH1, TASTEOFHOME.COM

BACON & SWISS CHICKEN SANDWICHES, 110

CHAPTER 4

SANDWICHES

Sandwiches! We love to dip, dunk, stack 'em and pack 'em. Here are some of our best—slow-cooked sammies, freshly baked calzones, and make-and-take party subs that'll star at the potluck.

CRISPY BUFFALO CHICKEN WRAPS

I'm big on wraps, even when I go out to eat. As a busy stay-at-home mom, I whip up this family favorite a lot. It's so good with chips and salsa on the side.
—*Christina Addison, Blanchester, OH*

. . . .

TAKES: 30 min. • **MAKES:** 4 servings

1 pkg. (12 oz.) frozen popcorn chicken
1 pkg. (8 oz.) shredded lettuce
2 medium tomatoes, finely chopped
1 cup shredded cheddar cheese
⅓ cup Buffalo wing sauce
4 flour tortillas (10 in.), warmed
Ranch or chipotle ranch salad dressing, optional

1. Cook chicken according to package directions; coarsely chop chicken. In a large bowl, mix chicken, lettuce, tomatoes and cheese. Drizzle with the wing sauce; toss to coat.

2. Spoon 1½ cups chicken mixture down center of each tortilla. Fold bottom of tortilla over filling; fold both sides to close. Serve immediately with salad dressing if desired.

1 WRAP: 570 cal., 26g fat (9g sat. fat), 55mg chol., 1895mg sod., 62g carb. (7g sugars, 4g fiber), 23g pro.

✱ READER RAVE

"Great idea to toss entire filling with the sauce—gave even more flavor! We added a pickle spear to each wrap to imitate a restaurant's version. Very quick and tasty dinner option."

—PPOLEN, TASTEOFHOME.COM

QUICK CALZONES

These hearty calzones look and taste like they're made from scratch. Frozen bread dough and jarred pasta sauce make them a snap to assemble. Add some cooked crumbled Italian sausage or pepperoni if you fancy it.

—Taste of Home *Test Kitchen*

TAKES: 30 min. • **MAKES:** 4 servings

1 loaf (1 lb.) frozen bread dough, thawed
1 cup pasta sauce with meat
¼ cup shredded part-skim mozzarella cheese
1 to 2 Tbsp. 2% milk
½ tsp. Italian seasoning
1 Tbsp. grated Parmesan cheese

1. Preheat oven to 350°. On a lightly floured surface, divide dough into four portions. Roll each into a 6-in. circle. Spread ¼ cup sauce over half of each circle to within ½ in. of edge; top with 1 Tbsp. mozzarella cheese. Fold dough over filling; pinch edges to seal. Place on a greased baking sheet.

2. Brush milk over tops; sprinkle with Italian seasoning and Parmesan cheese. Bake until golden brown, about 20-25 minutes.

1 CALZONE: 430 cal., 12g fat (3g sat. fat), 26mg chol., 1037mg sod., 63g carb. (6g sugars, 4g fiber), 21g pro.

SHRIMP PO'BOYS WITH PINEAPPLE SLAW

This twist on the traditional po'boy sandwich adds healthy veggies while reducing fat and calories. For a smoked flavor, grill the shrimp. For a low-carb option, serve the po'boy open-faced on a baguette half.

—Melissa Pelkey Hass, Waleska, GA

. . . .

TAKES: 30 min. • **MAKES:** 6 servings

- ⅓ cup egg substitute
- ½ cup panko (Japanese) bread crumbs
- 2 Tbsp. reduced-sodium Creole seasoning
- 1 lb. uncooked shrimp (16-20 per lb.), peeled and deveined
- 2 cups broccoli coleslaw mix
- 1 cup unsweetened pineapple tidbits, drained, 3 Tbsp. liquid reserved
- 2 green onions, chopped
- ½ cup reduced-fat mayonnaise
- 6 hoagie buns, split and toasted
- 4 Tbsp. fat-free tartar sauce
- 3 medium tomatoes, sliced

1. Preheat oven to 400°. Pour egg substitute into a shallow bowl. In a separate shallow bowl, mix bread crumbs and Creole seasoning. Dip shrimp in egg substitute, then in crumb mixture, patting to help coating adhere. Bake in a greased 15x10x1-in. pan until shrimp turn pink, 7-9 minutes. Keep warm.

2. Meanwhile, combine broccoli slaw, pineapple and green onions. In a small bowl, whisk together the mayonnaise and the reserved pineapple liquid until smooth. Add to broccoli mixture; toss to coat.

3. To serve, spread hoagie buns with tartar sauce. Divide tomato slices and shrimp among buns. Top with pineapple broccoli slaw.

1 SANDWICH: 420 cal., 13g fat (2g sat. fat), 99mg chol., 1430mg sod., 54g carb. (15g sugars, 3g fiber), 23g pro.

TUNA BURGERS

My family was so accustomed to a typical beef burger that they were hesitant to try these when I first made them. Any skepticism disappeared after one bite.
—*Kim Stoller, Smithville, OH*

TAKES: 20 min. • **MAKES:** 4 servings

1 large egg, lightly beaten
½ cup dry bread crumbs
½ cup finely chopped celery
⅓ cup mayonnaise
¼ cup finely chopped onion
2 Tbsp. chili sauce
1 pouch (6.4 oz.) light tuna in water
2 Tbsp. butter
4 hamburger buns, split and toasted
   Lettuce leaves and sliced tomato, optional

1. Mix first six ingredients; fold in tuna. Shape into four patties.

2. In a large skillet, heat butter over medium heat. Cook patties until lightly browned, 4-5 minutes per side. Serve on buns with lettuce and tomato if desired.

1 BURGER: 417 cal., 23g fat (7g sat. fat), 79mg chol., 710mg sod., 35g carb. (6g sugars, 2g fiber), 17g pro.

TURKEY FOCACCIA CLUB

My family thinks this sandwich is pure heaven, thanks to the cranberry-pecan mayo. It's so good, they ask me to make it all year long.
—*Judy Wilson, Sun City West, AZ*

TAKES: 20 min. • **MAKES:** 4 servings

½ cup mayonnaise
½ cup whole-berry cranberry sauce
2 Tbsp. chopped pecans, toasted
2 Tbsp. Dijon mustard
1 Tbsp. honey
1 loaf (8 oz.) focaccia bread
3 lettuce leaves
½ lb. thinly sliced cooked turkey
¼ lb. sliced Gouda cheese
8 slices tomato
6 bacon strips, cooked

In a small bowl, combine the first five ingredients. Using a long serrated knife, cut focaccia horizontally in half. Spread cut sides with mayonnaise mixture. Layer bottom half with lettuce, turkey, cheese, tomato and bacon; replace bread top. Cut into wedges.

NOTE: To toast nuts, bake them in a shallow pan in a 350° oven for 5-10 minutes or cook in a skillet over low heat until lightly browned, stirring occasionally.

1 WEDGE: 707 cal., 41g fat (10g sat. fat), 96mg chol., 1153mg sod., 53g carb. (17g sugars, 2g fiber), 32g pro.

BAVARIAN MEATBALL HOAGIES

When my husband's not working the grill, I count on my slow cooker.
These mouthwatering meatballs are just one reason why. They make a guaranteed
crowd-pleaser sandwich when spooned over crusty rolls and topped with cheese,
and they are irresistible served as appetizers, too.

—Peggy Rios, Mechanicsville, VA

PREP: 15 min. • **COOK:** 3 hours • **MAKES:** 12 servings

1 pkg. (32 oz.) frozen fully cooked Italian meatballs
½ cup chopped onion
¼ cup packed brown sugar
1 envelope onion soup mix
1 can (12 oz.) beer or nonalcoholic beer
12 hoagie buns, split
3 cups shredded Swiss cheese

1. In a 3-qt. slow cooker, combine meatballs, onion, brown sugar, soup mix and beer. Cook, covered, on low until meatballs are heated through, 3-4 hours.

2. Place five or six meatballs on each bun bottom. Sprinkle each sandwich with ¼ cup cheese. Place on baking sheets. Broil 4-6 in. from the heat until the cheese is melted, 2-3 minutes. Replace bun tops.

1 SANDWICH: 643 cal., 36g fat (18g sat. fat), 95mg chol., 1302mg sod., 49g carb. (13g sugars, 4g fiber), 29g pro.

LAYERED PICNIC LOAVES

This big sandwich is inspired by one I fell in love with at a New York deli. It's easy to make ahead of time and cart to any party. Kids and adults alike say it's super.
—*Marion Lowery, Medford, OR*

PREP: 20 min. + chilling • **MAKES:** 2 loaves (12 servings each)

2 unsliced loaves (1 lb. each) Italian bread
¼ cup olive oil
3 garlic cloves, minced
2 tsp. Italian seasoning, divided
½ lb. deli roast beef
12 slices part-skim mozzarella cheese (1 oz. each)
16 fresh basil leaves
3 medium tomatoes, thinly sliced
¼ lb. thinly sliced salami
1 jar (6½ oz.) marinated artichoke hearts, drained and sliced
1 pkg. (10 oz.) ready-to-serve salad greens
8 oz. thinly sliced deli chicken
1 medium onion, thinly sliced
¼ tsp. salt
⅛ tsp. pepper

1. Cut loaves in half horizontally; hollow out tops and bottoms, leaving ½-in. shells (discard removed bread or save for another use).

2. Combine oil and garlic; brush inside bread shells. Sprinkle with 1 tsp. Italian seasoning. Layer bottom of each loaf with a fourth of the roast beef, mozzarella, basil, tomatoes, salami, artichokes, salad greens, chicken and onion. Repeat layers. Season with salt, pepper and remaining Italian seasoning.

3. Drizzle with remaining oil mixture if desired. Replace bread tops; wrap tightly in plastic. Refrigerate loaves at least 1 hour before slicing.

1 SERVING: 341 cal., 18g fat (7g sat. fat), 47mg chol., 991mg sod., 26g carb. (3g sugars, 2g fiber), 19g pro.

SLOW COOKER
FRENCH DIP

For a sandwich with more pizzazz than the traditional French dip, give this recipe a try. The seasonings give the broth a wonderful flavor, and the meat cooks up tender and juicy. This sandwich will soon be a favorite at your house, like it is in mine.
—*Margaret McNeil, Germantown, TN*

PREP: 15 min. • **COOK:** 5 hours • **MAKES:** 8 servings

1 beef chuck roast (3 lbs.), trimmed
2 cups water
½ cup reduced-sodium soy sauce
1 tsp. dried rosemary, crushed
1 tsp. dried thyme
1 tsp. garlic powder
1 bay leaf
3 to 4 whole peppercorns
8 French rolls, split

1. Place roast in a 5-qt. slow cooker. Add the water, soy sauce and seasonings. Cover and cook roast on high for 5-6 hours or until beef is tender.

2. Remove meat from broth; shred with two forks and keep warm. Strain broth; skim fat. Pour broth into small cups for dipping. Serve beef on rolls.

1 SANDWICH: 467 cal., 19g fat (7g sat. fat), 111mg chol., 1300mg sod., 31g carb. (3g sugars, 2g fiber), 41g pro.

CARAMELIZED HAM & SWISS BUNS

My next-door neighbor shared her version of this recipe with me. You can make it ahead and cook it quickly when company arrives. The combo of poppy seeds, ham and cheese, horseradish and brown sugar makes it simply delicious!
—*Iris Weihemuller, Baxter, MN*

PREP: 25 min. + chilling • **BAKE:** 30 min. • **MAKES:** 1 dozen

1 pkg. (12 oz.) Hawaiian sweet rolls, split
½ cup horseradish sauce
12 slices deli ham
6 slices Swiss cheese, halved
½ cup butter, cubed
2 Tbsp. finely chopped onion
2 Tbsp. brown sugar
1 Tbsp. spicy brown mustard
2 tsp. poppy seeds
1½ tsp. Worcestershire sauce
¼ tsp. garlic powder

1. Spread roll bottoms with horseradish sauce. Layer with ham and cheese; replace tops. Arrange in a single layer in a greased 9-in. square baking pan.

2. In a small skillet, heat butter over medium-high heat. Add onion; cook and stir 1-2 minutes or until tender. Stir in remaining ingredients. Pour over rolls. Refrigerate, covered, several hours or overnight.

3. Preheat oven to 350°. Bake, covered, 25 minutes. Bake, uncovered, 5-10 minutes longer or until golden brown.

1 SANDWICH: 288 cal., 17g fat (9g sat. fat), 67mg chol., 447mg sod., 21g carb. (11g sugars, 1g fiber), 11g pro.

✳ TEST KITCHEN TIP

Turn this sandwich into a Reuben! Swap corned beef or pastrami for the ham, add a layer of sauerkraut and substitute caraway seeds for poppy.

TANGY PULLED PORK SANDWICHES

The slow cooker not only makes this an easy meal, but it keeps
the pork from drying out and builds the flavor. These sandwiches
are so comforting, especially with crunchy coleslaw.
—*Beki Kosydar-Krantz, Mayfield, PA*

PREP: 10 min. • **COOK:** 4 hours • **MAKES:** 4 servings

1 pork tenderloin (1 lb.)
1 cup ketchup
2 Tbsp. plus 1½ tsp. brown sugar
2 Tbsp. plus 1½ tsp. cider vinegar
1 Tbsp. plus 1½ tsp. Worcestershire sauce
1 Tbsp. spicy brown mustard
¼ tsp. pepper
4 rolls or buns, split and toasted
 Coleslaw, optional

1. Cut the tenderloin in half; place in a 3-qt. slow cooker. Combine the ketchup, brown sugar, vinegar, Worcestershire sauce, mustard and pepper; pour mixture over pork.

2. Cover and cook on low for 4-5 hours or until the meat is tender. Remove meat; shred with two forks. Return to the slow cooker; heat through. Serve on toasted rolls or buns, and, if desired, with coleslaw.

1 SANDWICH: 402 cal., 7g fat (2g sat. fat), 63mg chol., 1181mg sod., 56g carb. (18g sugars, 2g fiber), 29g pro.

✳ READER RAVE

"Delicious! I cannot wait to make this again. We quadrupled the recipe for our Memorial Day BBQ and it was a hit. Very tender, moist and flavorful sandwiches."

—CWYATT, TASTEOFHOME.COM

BACON & SWISS CHICKEN SANDWICHES

I created this sandwich based on one my daughter ordered at a restaurant.
She likes to dip hers in the extra honey-mustard sauce.

—*Marilyn Moberg, Papillion, NE*

TAKES: 25 min. • **MAKES:** 4 servings

¼ cup reduced-fat
mayonnaise
1 Tbsp. Dijon mustard
1 Tbsp. honey
4 boneless skinless
chicken breast halves
(4 oz. each)
½ tsp. Montreal steak
seasoning
4 slices Swiss cheese
4 whole wheat
hamburger buns, split
2 bacon strips, cooked
and crumbled
Lettuce leaves and
tomato slices, optional

1. In a small bowl, mix mayonnaise, mustard and honey. Pound chicken with a meat mallet to ½-in. thickness. Sprinkle chicken with steak seasoning. Grill chicken, covered, over medium heat or broil 4 in. from heat 4-6 minutes on each side or until a thermometer reads 165°. Top with cheese during the last 1 minute of cooking.

2. Grill buns over medium heat, cut side down, for 30-60 seconds or until toasted. Serve chicken on buns with the bacon, mayonnaise mixture and, if desired, lettuce and tomato.

1 SANDWICH: 410 cal., 17g fat (6g sat. fat), 91mg chol., 667mg sod., 29g carb. (9g sugars, 3g fiber), 34g pro. *Diabetic exchanges:* 4 lean meat, 2 starch, 2 fat.

MOZZARELLA BEEF ROLL-UPS

The kids will love these pepperoni and beef wraps. They're easy to assemble because each tortilla is simply wrapped around a portion of hearty meat filling and a piece of string cheese.
—Taste of Home *Test Kitchen*

TAKES: 30 min. • **MAKES:** 6 servings

1 lb. ground beef
1 medium green pepper, chopped
⅓ cup chopped onion
1 can (8 oz.) pizza sauce
2 oz. sliced pepperoni (about ⅔ cup)
½ tsp. dried oregano
6 flour tortillas (10 in.), warmed
6 pieces string cheese (about 6 oz.)

1. Preheat oven to 350°. In a large skillet, cook and crumble beef with pepper and onion over medium-high heat until no longer pink, 5-7 minutes; drain. Stir in pizza sauce, pepperoni and oregano.

2. Spoon ½ cup mixture across center of each tortilla; top with a string cheese. Fold bottom and sides of tortilla over filling and roll up.

3. Place on an ungreased baking sheet, seam side down. Bake until heated through, about 10 minutes.

FREEZE OPTION: Cool beef mixture before assembly. Individually wrap roll-ups in foil and freeze in a resealable plastic freezer bag. To use, partially thaw overnight in refrigerator. Reheat foil-wrapped roll-ups on a baking sheet in a preheated 350° oven until heated through. To reheat individually, remove foil and rewrap in paper towel; place on a microwave-safe plate. Microwave on high until heated through, turning once. Let stand 15 seconds.

1 ROLL-UP: 513 cal., 25g fat (11g sat. fat), 71mg chol., 1064mg sod., 41g carb. (5g sugars, 4g fiber), 30g pro.

BEER-BRAISED PULLED HAM

To jazz up leftover ham, I slow-cooked it with a beer sauce. Buns loaded with ham, pickles and mustard make the pulled ham irresistible.
—*Ann Sheehy, Lawrence, MA*

PREP: 10 min. • **COOK:** 7 hours • **MAKES:** 16 servings

2 bottles (12 oz. each) beer or nonalcoholic beer
¾ cup German or Dijon mustard, divided
½ tsp. coarsely ground pepper
1 fully cooked bone-in ham (about 4 lbs.)
4 fresh rosemary sprigs
16 pretzel hamburger buns, split
Dill pickle slices, optional

1. In a 5-qt. slow cooker, whisk together beer and ½ cup mustard. Stir in pepper. Add ham and rosemary. Cook, covered, on low until ham is tender, 7-9 hours.

2. Remove ham; cool slightly. Discard rosemary sprigs. Skim fat. When ham is cool enough to handle, shred the meat with two forks. Discard bone. Return to slow cooker; heat through.

3. Using tongs, place shredded ham on pretzel buns; top with remaining mustard and, if desired, pickles.

FREEZE OPTION: Freeze cooled ham mixture in freezer containers. To use, partially thaw the ham in refrigerator overnight. Heat through in a covered saucepan, stirring gently and adding a little water if necessary.

1 SANDWICH: 378 cal., 9g fat (1g sat. fat), 50mg chol., 1246mg sod., 48g carb. (4g sugars, 2g fiber), 25g pro.

✱ TEST KITCHEN TIP

You can also place shredded ham on slider buns and top them with honey-mustard spread.

**BASIL PORK
CHOPS, 137**

CHAPTER 5

MAIN COURSES

From crowd-pleasing ham to bubbly stuffed shells, simple slow-cooked pot roast and sensational grilled halibut, you will love discovering (and sharing!) these best-loved main dishes.

SLOW-SIMMERED MEAT RAGU

After a day of simmering in the slow cooker, this ragu is not your typical spaghetti sauce. It's so hearty, it's almost like a stew.
—*Laurie LaClair, North Richland Hills, TX*

PREP: 30 min. • **COOK:** 6 hours • **MAKES:** 10 servings

1 jar (24 oz.) tomato basil pasta sauce
1 can (14½ oz.) Italian diced tomatoes, undrained
2 jars (6 oz. each) sliced mushrooms, drained
1 can (8 oz.) tomato sauce
1 jar (3½ oz.) prepared pesto
1½ lbs. chicken tenderloins
1 medium sweet red pepper, chopped
½ cup chopped pepperoni
½ cup pitted ripe olives, halved
1 tsp. dried oregano
½ tsp. hot pepper sauce
1 lb. Italian sausage links, cut into 1-in. pieces
1 medium onion, chopped
  Hot cooked angel hair pasta

1. In a 5- or 6-qt. slow cooker, combine the first 11 ingredients. Heat a large skillet over medium heat. Add sausage and onion; cook and stir until sausage is no longer pink and onion is tender. Drain. Add to slow cooker.

2. Cook, covered, on low 6-8 hours or until chicken is tender. Serve with pasta.

FREEZE OPTION: Do not cook or add pasta. Freeze cooled sauce in freezer containers. To use, partially thaw in refrigerator overnight. Cook pasta according to package directions. Place meat mixture in a large saucepan; heat through, stirring occasionally and adding a little water if necessary. Proceed as directed.

1 CUP RAGU: 341 cal., 20g fat (5g sat. fat), 64mg chol., 1294mg sod., 18g carb. (10g sugars, 4g fiber), 26g pro.

LEMON-DILL SALMON PACKETS

Grilling in foil is an easy technique I use with foods
that cook quickly, like fish, shrimp, bite-sized meats and
fresh veggies. The options are endless—and the cleanup is easy.
—*A.J. Weinhold, McArthur, CA*

TAKES: 25 min. • **MAKES:** 4 servings

1 Tbsp. butter, softened
4 salmon fillets
   (6 oz. each)
½ tsp. salt
¼ tsp. pepper
½ medium onion, sliced
4 garlic cloves, sliced
4 fresh dill sprigs
1 Tbsp. minced fresh basil
1 medium lemon, sliced

1. Prepare campfire or grill for medium heat. Spread butter in the center of each of four pieces of a double thickness of foil (about 12 in. square). Place one salmon fillet in the center of each; sprinkle with salt and pepper. Top with onion, garlic, dill, basil and lemon. Fold foil around fillets; seal.

2. Place packets on a grill grate over a campfire or grill. Cook 8-10 minutes or until fish just begins to flake easily with a fork. Open carefully to allow the steam to escape.

1 FILLET: 305 cal., 19g fat (5g sat. fat), 93mg chol., 405mg sod., 4g carb. (1g sugars, 1g fiber), 29g pro. *Diabetic exchanges:* 5 lean meat, 1 fat.

FLAVORFUL POT ROAST

This is so quick and easy to prep! Convenient packages of dressing and gravy combine to create delicious sauce for a fall-apart roast. It's perfect for large family get-togethers.
—*Arlene Butler, Ogden, UT*

PREP: 10 min. • **COOK:** 7 hours • **MAKES:** 15 servings

- **2** boneless beef chuck roasts (2½ lbs. each)
- **1** envelope ranch salad dressing mix
- **1** envelope Italian salad dressing mix
- **1** envelope brown gravy mix
- **½** cup water
  Chopped fresh parsley, optional

Place the chuck roasts in a 5-qt. slow cooker. In a small bowl, combine the salad dressings and gravy mix; stir in water. Pour over meat. Cover and cook on low for 7-8 hours or until tender. If desired, sprinkle with the parsley and thicken cooking juices for gravy.

4 OZ. COOKED BEEF: 142 cal., 7g fat (3g sat. fat), 49mg chol., 496mg sod., 3g carb. (1g sugars, 0 fiber), 15g pro.

FOLD-OVER TORTILLA BAKE

Here's something a little different from the usual tacos.
It's special enough for potlucks or dinner guests.
—*Deborah Smith, DeWitt, NE*

PREP: 20 min. • **BAKE:** 20 min. • **MAKES:** 6 servings

1 lb. ground beef
1 cup chopped onion
2 cans (14½ oz. each) stewed tomatoes
1 cup enchilada sauce
1 to 2 tsp. ground cumin
½ tsp. salt
¼ tsp. pepper
12 flour or corn tortillas (6 in.)
6 oz. cream cheese, softened
1 can (4 oz.) chopped green chilies, drained
1 cup shredded Monterey Jack cheese
Minced fresh cilantro, optional

1. In a large skillet, cook ground beef and onion until beef is no longer pink; drain. Stir in the tomatoes, enchilada sauce and seasonings. Bring to a boil. Reduce heat and simmer, covered, for 5 minutes. Pour half of the meat sauce into a 13x9-in. baking dish. Set aside.

2. Wrap the stack of tortillas in foil; warm at 350° for 8-10 minutes. Spread warm tortillas with cream cheese and top with the chilies. Fold tortillas in half. Arrange folded tortillas over meat sauce; pour remaining sauce over top.

3. Cover and bake at 350° for 15 minutes. Sprinkle with cheese; bake 5 minutes longer or until cheese is melted. If desired, top with cilantro.

2 TORTILLAS : 473 cal., 25g fat (10g sat. fat), 69mg chol., 1138mg sod., 38g carb. (7g sugars, 2g fiber), 27g pro.

SWEET TEA BARBECUED CHICKEN

Marinades sometimes use coffee or espresso, and that
inspired me to add tea to perk up a barbecue sauce.
—*Kelly Williams, Forked River, NJ*

PREP: 15 min. • **COOK:** 1 hour • **MAKES:** 8 servings

1 cup unsweetened
  apple juice
1 cup water
2 tsp. seafood seasoning
1 tsp. paprika
1 tsp. garlic powder
1 tsp. coarsely ground
  pepper
1 chicken (4 to 5 lbs.),
  cut up
1 cup barbecue sauce
½ cup sweet tea

1. Preheat oven to 350°. Pour apple juice and water into a large shallow roasting pan. Mix the seafood seasoning, paprika, garlic powder and pepper; rub over chicken. Place in roasting pan.

2. Bake, covered, until the chicken juices run clear and a thermometer reads 170° to 175°, for about 50-60 minutes. Transfer the chicken to a foil-lined 15x10x1-in. baking pan. Whisk barbecue sauce and sweet tea; brush some of mixture over chicken.

3. Place chicken on greased grill rack; grill over medium heat 3-4 minutes per side, brushing occasionally with remaining sauce.

1 SERVING: 374 cal., 17g fat (5g sat. fat), 104mg chol., 608mg sod., 19g carb. (16g sugars, 1g fiber), 33g pro.

ITALIAN STUFFED SHELLS

A dear friend first brought over this casserole. Now I take it to other friends' homes and to potlucks, because it's always a big hit!
—*Beverly Austin, Fulton, MO*

PREP: 50 min. • **BAKE:** 35 min. • **MAKES:** 8 servings

1 lb. ground beef
1 cup chopped onion
1 garlic clove, minced
2 cups hot water
1 can (12 oz.) tomato paste
1 Tbsp. beef bouillon granules
1½ tsp. dried oregano
1 large egg, lightly beaten
2 cups 4% cottage cheese
2 cups shredded part-skim mozzarella cheese, divided
½ cup grated Parmesan cheese
24 jumbo pasta shells, cooked and drained

1. In a large skillet, cook beef, onion and garlic over medium heat, crumbling beef, until meat is no longer pink; drain. Stir in water, tomato paste, bouillon and oregano. Reduce the heat; simmer, uncovered, for 30 minutes.

2. Meanwhile, combine egg, cottage cheese, 1 cup mozzarella and Parmesan cheese. Stuff shells with cheese mixture.

3. Preheat oven to 350°. Arrange shells in a greased 13x9-in. or 3-qt. baking dish. Pour meat sauce over shells. Cover; bake 30 minutes. Uncover; sprinkle with remaining mozzarella cheese. Bake until cheese is melted, about 5 minutes longer.

FREEZE OPTION: After assembling, cover and freeze. To use, partially thaw in refrigerator overnight. Remove 30 minutes before baking. Preheat oven to 350°. Bake as directed, adding remaining 1 cup mozzarella after 30-40 minutes and increasing time as necessary for a thermometer inserted in center to read 165°.

3 STUFFED SHELLS AND SAUCE: 430 cal., 17g fat (8g sat. fat), 94mg chol., 866mg sod., 37g carb. (9g sugars, 3g fiber), 32g pro.

GINGER HALIBUT WITH BRUSSELS SPROUTS

I moved to the United States from Russia and love cooking Russian food for family and friends. Halibut with soy sauce, ginger and pepper is a favorite.
—*Margarita Parker, New Bern, NC*

TAKES: 25 min. • **MAKES:** 4 servings

4 tsp. lemon juice
4 halibut fillets
   (4 to 6 oz. each)
1 tsp. minced fresh
   gingerroot
¼ to ¾ tsp. salt, divided
¼ tsp. pepper
½ cup water
10 oz. (about 2½ cups)
   fresh Brussels sprouts,
   halved
   Crushed red pepper
   flakes
1 Tbsp. canola oil
5 garlic cloves, sliced
   lengthwise
2 Tbsp. sesame oil
2 Tbsp. soy sauce
   Lemon slices, optional

1. Brush lemon juice over halibut fillets. Sprinkle with minced ginger, ¼ tsp. salt and pepper.

2. Place fish on an oiled grill rack, skin side down. Grill, covered, over medium heat (or broil 6 in. from heat) until the fish just begins to flake easily with a fork, 6-8 minutes.

3. In a large skillet, bring water to a boil over medium-high heat. Add Brussels sprouts, pepper flakes and, if desired, remaining salt. Cook, covered, until tender, 5-7 minutes. Meanwhile, in a small skillet, heat oil over medium heat. Add garlic; cook until golden brown. Drain on paper towels.

4. Drizzle sesame oil and soy sauce over halibut. Serve with the Brussels sprouts; sprinkle with fried garlic. If desired, serve with lemon slices.

1 FILLET WITH ½ CUP BRUSSELS SPROUTS: 234 cal., 12g fat (2g sat. fat), 56mg chol., 701mg sod., 7g carb. (2g sugars, 3g fiber), 24g pro. *Diabetic exchanges:* 3 lean meat, 2 fat, 1 vegetable.

SKILLET MAC & CHEESE

This super creamy mac 'n' cheese is so simple it seems almost too easy! Kids really go for the rich cheese flavor, but I've never met an adult who didn't love it, too.
—*Ann Bowers, Rockport, TX*

TAKES: 25 min. • **MAKES:** 4 servings

2 cups uncooked elbow macaroni (about 8 oz.)
2 Tbsp. butter
2 Tbsp. all-purpose flour
1½ cups half-and-half cream
¾ lb. process cheese (Velveeta), cubed
Fresh arugula, halved cherry tomatoes and coarsely ground pepper, optional

1. Cook macaroni according to package directions; drain.

2. Meanwhile, in a large nonstick skillet, melt butter over medium heat. Stir in flour until smooth; gradually whisk in cream. Bring to a boil, stirring constantly. Cook and stir until thickened, about 2 minutes. Reduce heat; stir in cheese until melted.

3. Add macaroni; cook and stir until heated through. Top as desired.

1½ CUPS: 600 cal., 37g fat (23g sat. fat), 144mg chol., 1185mg sod., 40g carb. (9g sugars, 1g fiber), 23g pro.

PIEROGI BEEF SKILLET

Hearty and thick with beef, veggies and potatoes, this is a complete meal in one.
—Taste of Home *Test Kitchen*

....

TAKES: 25 min. • **MAKES:** 4 servings

1   lb. ground beef
½   cup chopped onion
¼   cup all-purpose flour
½   tsp. Italian seasoning
½   tsp. pepper
⅛   tsp. salt
1   can (14½ oz.) beef broth
1   pkg. (16 oz.) frozen cheese and potato pierogies, thawed
2   cups frozen mixed vegetables (about 10 oz.), thawed and drained
½   cup shredded cheddar cheese

1. In a large skillet, cook and crumble beef with onion over medium heat until no longer pink, 5-7 minutes; drain, reserving 3 Tbsp. drippings. Stir in flour and seasonings until blended. Gradually stir in broth; bring to a boil. Cook and stir until thickened, 1-2 minutes.

2. Stir in pierogies and vegetables. Cook, uncovered, until heated through, about 5 minutes, stirring mixture occasionally. Sprinkle with cheese.

1¾ CUPS: 654 cal., 31g fat (12g sat. fat), 102mg chol., 1157mg sod., 57g carb. (12g sugars, 7g fiber), 34g pro.

✱ DID YOU KNOW?

Pierogi, little stuffed half-moon-shaped dumplings, are Poland's national dish. They are especially popular in the American northeast, the upper Midwest and in Canada. Although Polish people call them simply pierogi, North Americans like to call them pierogies to emphasize the idea of eating more than just one!

BASIL PORK CHOPS

These tender chops get a kick of flavor from basil, chili powder and a little brown sugar. When you serve them with your favorite roasted veggies, you've got a super comforting meal bursting with flavor.
—*Lisa Gilliland, Fort Collins, CO*

TAKES: 25 min. • **MAKES:** 4 servings

¼ cup packed brown sugar
1½ tsp. dried basil
½ tsp. salt
½ tsp. chili powder
2 Tbsp. canola oil, divided
4 boneless pork loin chops (½ in. thick and 4 oz. each)

1. Mix first four ingredients; gradually stir in 1 Tbsp. oil (mixture will be crumbly). Rub over both sides of pork chops.

2. In a large skillet, heat remaining oil over medium heat; cook pork chops until a thermometer reads 145°, 4-6 minutes per side. Let stand for 5 minutes before serving.

1 PORK CHOP: 152 cal., 8g fat (1g sat. fat), 14mg chol., 312mg sod., 14g carb. (13g sugars, 0 fiber), 6g p

✱ READER RAVE

"I substitute olive oil for the canola oil. I made it using paprika as I was out of chili powder. My mother-in-law, husband, and sons (16, 15 and 5) all loved it. Another time, I was in a bind and needed something ready for when we got home from the gym, so I threw it in the slow cooker on high for 1 hour 30 minutes...will definitely keep making this."
—TIGERZESCHY, TASTEOFHOME.COM

SWEET & SAVORY BRISKET

I like this recipe because it makes such tender and flavorful beef. And it's wonderful to come home from work and have such a mouthwatering dish waiting for you.
—*Chris Snyder, Boulder, CO*

PREP: 10 min. • **COOK:** 8 hours • **MAKES:** 10 servings

1 beef brisket (3 to 3½ lbs.), cut in half
1 cup ketchup
¼ cup grape jelly
1 envelope onion soup mix
½ tsp. pepper

1. Place half of the brisket in a 5-qt. slow cooker. In a small bowl, combine the ketchup, jelly, soup mix and pepper; spread half over meat. Top with the remaining meat and ketchup mixture.

2. Cover and cook on low for 8-10 hours or until meat is tender. Slice brisket; serve with cooking juice.

NOTE: This is a fresh beef brisket, not corned beef.

4 OZ. COOKED BEEF: 223 cal., 6g fat (2g sat. fat), 58mg chol., 596mg sod., 13g carb. (11g sugars, 0 fiber), 28g pro. *Diabetic exchanges:* 4 lean meat, 1 starch.

SAUSAGE HASH

We always have plenty of pork sausage around, so when I need a quick supper, I use this handy recipe. The colorful vegetables give the hash a bold look to match its flavor.

— Virginia Krites, Cridersville, OH

PREP: 10 min. • **COOK:** 30 min. • **MAKES:** 6 servings

- 1 lb. bulk pork sausage
- 1 medium onion, chopped
- 2 medium carrots, grated
- 1 medium green pepper, chopped
- 3 cups diced cooked potatoes
- ½ tsp. salt
- ¼ tsp. pepper

In a large skillet, cook the sausage over medium heat until no longer pink; drain. Add the onion, carrots and green pepper; cook until tender. Stir in potatoes, salt and pepper. Reduce heat; cook and stir 20 minutes or until lightly browned.

1 SERVING: 245 cal., 14g fat (5g sat. fat), 27mg chol., 519mg sod., 22g carb. (5g sugars, 3g fiber), 8g pro.

✱ READER RAVE

"Used Italian sausage, and used spinach instead of green pepper. Also served with a fried egg on top. This was a delicious, quick weeknight meal!"

LOTS_A_SMILES, TASTEOFHOME.COM

SUGAR-GLAZED HAM

An old-fashioned sugar glaze gives your ham a pretty, golden-brown coating just like Grandma used to make. The mustard and vinegar complement the brown sugar and add tangy flavor. Be prepared to serve seconds!

—Carol Strong Battle, Heathsville, VA

PREP: 5 min. • **BAKE:** 1¾ hours • **MAKES:** 14 servings

1 fully cooked bone-in ham (5 to 7 lbs.)
1 cup packed brown sugar
2 tsp. prepared mustard
1 to 2 Tbsp. cider vinegar

1. Preheat oven to 325°. Place the ham on a rack in a shallow roasting pan. Using a sharp knife, score surface of ham with ¼-in.-deep cuts in a diamond pattern. Cover and bake 1½ to 2 hours or until a thermometer reads 130°.

2. Meanwhile, in a small bowl, combine the brown sugar, mustard and enough vinegar to make a thick paste. Remove ham from oven. Spread sugar mixture over ham. Bake ham, uncovered, 15-30 minutes longer or until a thermometer reads 140°.

4 OZ. HAM: 284 cal., 16g fat (6g sat. fat), 57mg chol., 1110mg sod., 15g carb. (15g sugars, 0 fiber), 20g pro.

FAJITA IN A
BOWL, 170

CHAPTER 6

SIDES & SALADS

Garden-fresh salads and side dishes highlight the best that each season has to offer. From berry-kissed spring salads to maple-glazed winter squash, you'll discover delicious meal ideas here.

CORN PUDDING

The pleasing flavor of this golden corn pudding side dish makes it real comfort food. And because the recipe calls for a packaged corn mix, it's easy to prepare.
—*P. Lauren Fay-Neri, Syracuse, NY*

PREP: 20 min. • **BAKE:** 45 min. • **MAKES:** 8 servings

½ cup butter, softened
½ cup sugar
2 large eggs
1 cup sour cream
1 pkg. (8½ oz.) cornbread/ muffin mix
½ cup 2% milk
1 can (15¼ oz.) whole kernel corn, drained
1 can (14¾ oz.) cream- style corn

1. Preheat oven to 325°. In a large bowl, cream butter and sugar until light and fluffy. Add eggs, one at a time, beating well after each addition. Beat in sour cream. Gradually add the muffin mix alternately with milk. Fold in corn.

2. Pour into a greased 3-qt. baking dish or 13x9-in. baking pan. Bake, uncovered, 45-50 minutes or until set and lightly browned.

¾ CUP: 435 cal., 22g fat (12g sat. fat), 112mg chol., 700mg sod., 52g carb. (24g sugars, 2g fiber), 7g pro.

OLD-FASHIONED GREEN BEANS

Mom would prepare home-grown green beans using this recipe, and boy did they ever taste good. The bacon provides rich flavor and the brown sugar a touch of sweetness. This is one irresistible side dish.
—*Willa Govoro, St. Clair, MO*

TAKES: 30 min. • **MAKES:** 6-8 servings

6 bacon strips, cut into ½-in. pieces
2 lbs. fresh green beans
3 Tbsp. brown sugar
½ cup water

In a large skillet, cook bacon over medium heat until crisp, about 5 minutes. Add beans, brown sugar and water. Stir gently; bring to a boil. Reduce heat; cover and simmer for 15 minutes or until beans are crisp-tender. Remove to a serving dish with a slotted spoon.

¾ CUP: 145 cal., 10g fat (4g sat. fat), 11mg chol., 132mg sod., 12g carb. (8g sugars, 3g fiber), 3g pro.

✱ TEST KITCHEN TIP

Instead of snapping off the ends of each green bean, trim a bunch in seconds. Gather beans in a small pile, lining up the tips on one side. Cut off tips with a single slice using a chef's knife.

DAD'S GREEK SALAD

The heart of a Greek salad is the olives, feta and fresh veggies.
Dress it with oil and vinegar, then add olives and cheese.
—*Arge Salvatori, Waldwick, NJ*

TAKES: 20 min. • **MAKES:** 8 servings

4 large tomatoes, seeded and coarsely chopped
2½ cups thinly sliced English cucumbers
1 small red onion, halved and thinly sliced
¼ cup olive oil
3 Tbsp. red wine vinegar
¼ tsp. salt
⅛ tsp. pepper
¼ tsp. dried oregano, optional
¾ cup pitted Greek olives
¾ cup crumbled feta cheese

Place tomatoes, cucumbers and onion in a large bowl. In a small bowl, whisk oil, vinegar, salt and pepper and, if desired, oregano until blended. Drizzle over salad; toss to coat. Top with olives and cheese.

¾ CUP: 148 cal., 12g fat (2g sat. fat), 6mg chol., 389mg sod., 7g carb. (3g sugars, 2g fiber), 3g pro. *Diabetic exchanges:* 2 vegetable, 2 fat.

GARLIC PEPPER CORN

I've loved corn served with this simple seasoning since I was a child.
It's so simple, but it makes corn on the cob extra special.
—*Anna Minegar, Zolfo Springs, FL*

TAKES: 25 min. • **MAKES:** 8 servings

1 Tbsp. dried parsley
flakes

1 Tbsp. garlic pepper
blend

½ tsp. paprika

¼ tsp. salt

8 medium ears sweet
corn, husked

¼ cup butter, melted

1. In a small bowl, combine the parsley, garlic pepper, paprika and salt; set aside. Place corn in a Dutch oven; cover with water. Bring to a boil; cover and cook corn for 3 minutes or until tender. Drain.

2. Brush the corn with butter; sprinkle ears with the seasoning mixture.

1 EAR OF CORN: 128 cal., 7g fat (4g sat. fat), 15mg chol., 251mg sod., 17g carb. (5g sugars, 2g fiber), 3g pro. *Diabetic exchanges:* 1 starch, 1 fat.

BALSAMIC ZUCCHINI SAUTE

This superfast vegetarian dish is flavorful and only uses a few ingredients,
so it's easy to whip up as your entree is cooking.
—Elizabeth Bramkamp, Gig Harbor, WA

TAKES: 20 min. • **MAKES:** 4 servings

1 Tbsp. olive oil
3 medium zucchini, cut into thin slices
½ cup chopped sweet onion
½ tsp. salt
½ tsp. dried rosemary, crushed
¼ tsp. pepper
2 Tbsp. balsamic vinegar
⅓ cup crumbled feta cheese

In a large skillet, heat oil over medium-high heat; saute zucchini and onion until crisp-tender, 6-8 minutes. Stir in seasonings. Add vinegar; cook and stir 2 minutes. Top with cheese.

½ CUP: 94 cal., 5g fat (2g sat. fat), 5mg chol., 398mg sod., 9g carb. (6g sugars, 2g fiber), 4g pro. *Diabetic exchanges: 1 vegetable, 1 fat.*

SLOW-COOKER MASHED POTATOES

Sour cream and cream cheese give richness to these smooth make-ahead potatoes. They are wonderful for Thanksgiving or Christmas dinner since there's no last-minute mashing required.

— Trudy Vincent, Valles Mines, MO

PREP: 20 min. • **COOK:** 2 hours • **MAKES:** 10 servings

- 3 oz. cream cheese, softened
- ½ cup sour cream
- ¼ cup plus 1 Tbsp. softened butter, divided
- 1 envelope ranch salad dressing mix
- 1 Tbsp. minced fresh parsley
- 6 cups warm mashed potatoes (without added milk or butter)

In a large bowl, combine the cream cheese, sour cream, ¼ cup butter, salad dressing mix and parsley; stir in the mashed potatoes. Transfer to a 3-qt. slow cooker. Cover and cook on low for 2-3 hours. Top with remaining butter.

¾ cup: 210 cal., 11g fat (7g sat. fat), 27mg chol., 670mg sod., 23g carb. (1g sugars, 4g fiber), 3g pro.

BERRY-BEET SALAD

Here's a delightfully different salad that balances the earthy flavor of beets with the tart sweetness of berries. If you prefer, substitute crumbled feta for the goat cheese.
—*Amy Lyons, Mounds View, MN*

PREP: 20 min. • **BAKE:** 30 min. + cooling • **MAKES:** 4 servings

1 red beet
1 golden beet
¼ cup balsamic vinegar
2 Tbsp. walnut oil
1 tsp. honey
   Dash salt
   Dash pepper
½ cup sliced fresh strawberries
½ cup fresh raspberries
½ cup fresh blackberries
3 Tbsp. chopped walnuts, toasted
1 shallot, thinly sliced
4 cups torn mixed salad greens
1 oz. fresh goat cheese, crumbled
1 Tbsp. fresh basil, thinly sliced

1. Place beets in an 8-in. square baking dish; add 1 in. of water. Cover and bake at 400° for 30-40 minutes or until tender.

2. Meanwhile, in a small bowl, whisk the vinegar, oil, honey, salt and pepper; set aside. Cool beets; peel and cut into thin slices.

3. In a large bowl, combine the beets, berries, walnuts and shallot. Pour dressing over beet mixture and toss gently to coat. Divide salad greens among four plates. Top with beet mixture; sprinkle with cheese and basil.

1 SERVING: 183 cal., 12g fat (2g sat. fat), 5mg chol., 124mg sod., 18g carb. (11g sugars, 5g fiber), 4g pro. *Diabetic exchanges:* 2 fat, 1 starch.

BLUE CHEESE & GRAPE COLESLAW

Dishes like coleslaw beg for a fresh approach. I update mine with almonds, grapes, blue cheese and bacon for a grand bowl of flavor and crunch.
—*Jeannine Bunge, Hartley, IA*

PREP: 20 min. + chilling • **MAKES:** 8 servings

1 pkg. (14 oz.) coleslaw mix
¾ cup sliced almonds, toasted
¾ cup quartered green grapes
¾ cup quartered seedless red grapes
½ cup crumbled blue cheese
3 bacon strips, cooked and crumbled
¼ tsp. pepper
¾ cup coleslaw salad dressing

Combine first seven ingredients. Pour dressing over salad; toss to coat. Refrigerate 1 hour.

NOTE: To toast nuts, bake in a shallow pan in a 350° oven for 5-10 minutes or cook in a skillet over low heat until lightly browned, stirring occasionally.

¾ CUP: 212 cal., 15g fat (3g sat. fat), 17mg chol., 339mg sod., 16g carb. (12g sugars, 3g fiber), 5g pro.

✳ TEST KITCHEN TIP

To make quick work of the salad prep, use an egg slicer to slice several grapes at a time, rather than cutting each into wedges.

MAPLE-GLAZED ACORN SQUASH

With a maple syrup and brown sugar glaze, acorn squash becomes pleasantly sweet. This is real comfort food—easy to prepare and a tasty pairing with a pork entree.

—Nancy Mueller, Menomonee Falls, WI

PREP: 10 min. • **BAKE:** 55 min. • **MAKES:** 2 servings

1   medium acorn squash, halved
¾   cup water
¼   cup maple syrup
2   Tbsp. brown sugar
½   tsp. ground cinnamon
¼   tsp. ground ginger
¼   tsp. salt

1. Preheat oven to 350°. Scoop out and discard seeds from squash. Place cut side down in a 13x9-in. baking dish; add water. Bake, uncovered, for 45 minutes.

2. If necessary, drain water from pan; turn squash cut side up. Combine syrup, brown sugar, cinnamon, ginger and salt; pour into squash halves. Bake the squash, uncovered, for 10 minutes or until glaze is heated through.

½ SQUASH: 251 cal., 0 fat (0 sat. fat), 0 chol., 311mg sod., 65g carb. (43g sugars, 4g fiber), 2g pro.

END OF GARDEN RELISH

We dollop this tangy relish on burgers, hot dogs and salads. It's a cool way to use up garden produce and is always appreciated at picnics and potlucks.
—*Karen Stucky, Freeman, SD*

PREP: 45 min. + standing • **PROCESS:** 20 min. • **MAKES:** 6 pints

7 large cucumbers, shredded
3 large onions, finely chopped
3 cups shredded carrots
2 medium sweet red peppers, finely chopped
5 Tbsp. salt
5 cups sugar
3 cups white vinegar
1 Tbsp. celery seed
1 Tbsp. mustard seed

1. Toss first five ingredients; let stand 3 hours. Drain; squeeze and blot dry with paper towels.

2. In a Dutch oven, mix sugar, vinegar, celery seed and mustard seed; bring to a boil. Reduce heat; simmer, uncovered, 5 minutes. Add vegetables; bring to a boil. Reduce heat; simmer, uncovered, 20 minutes.

3. Ladle hot mixture into hot 1-pint jars, leaving ½-in. headspace. Remove air bubbles and adjust headspace, if necessary, by adding hot mixture. Wipe rims. Center lids on jars; screw on bands until fingertip tight.

4. Place the jars into canner with simmering water, ensuring that they are completely covered with water. Bring to a boil; process for 20 minutes. Remove jars and cool.

NOTE: The processing time listed is for altitudes of 1,000 feet or less. For altitudes up to 3,000 feet, add 5 minutes; 6,000 feet, add 10 minutes; 8,000 feet, add 15 minutes; 10,000 feet, add 20 minutes.

2 TABLESPOONS: 8 cal., 0 fat (0 sat. fat), 0 chol., 7mg sod., 2g carb. (1g sugars, 0 fiber), 0 pro.

SLOW-COOKED BEAN MEDLEY

I often change the variety of beans in this classic recipe, using whatever I have on hand to total the 5 cans called for. The sauce makes any combination delicious! It's a gluten-free side dish that's popular with just about everyone.
—*Peggy Gwillim, Strasbourg, , SK*

PREP: 25 min. • **COOK:** 5 hours • **MAKES:** 12 servings (¾ cup each)

1½ cups ketchup
2 celery ribs, chopped
1 medium onion, chopped
1 medium green pepper, chopped
1 medium sweet red pepper, chopped
½ cup packed brown sugar
½ cup water
½ cup Italian salad dressing
2 bay leaves
1 Tbsp. cider vinegar
1 tsp. ground mustard
⅛ tsp. pepper
5 cans (15-16 oz.) beans, rinsed and drained (kidney, great northern, lima, black, and black-eyed peas)
1 can (15¼ oz.) whole kernel corn, drained

In a 5-qt. slow cooker, combine the first 12 ingredients. Stir in the remaining ingredients. Cover and cook on low for 5-6 hours or until the onion and peppers are tender. Discard bay leaves.

¾ CUP: 255 cal., 4g fat (0 sat. fat), 0 chol., 942mg sod., 45g carb. (21g sugars, 7g fiber), 9g pro.

✶ READER RAVE

"For a church potluck, I swapped out lima beans and black-eyed peas for: Mexican corn (I drained) and a can of chili beans with garlic, onion and peppers (which I didn't drain). I didn't add water. I only used 1 cup ketchup, ¼ cup brown sugar and used 1 yellow pepper instead of green. I used 1 cup each of cooked, chopped bacon & ham. Next time I will try it with hamburger. Everyone raved about this dish, so I had to give it 5 stars!"

—CARLAHARDENBROOK, TASTEOFHOME.COM

DILLY POTATO & EGG SALAD

Everyone has a favorite potato salad, and this is mine. As a young bride, I was eager to learn how to cook and make things that my husband would love. And so I combined my mom's and his mom's recipes, and this is the delicious result.
—*Angela Leinenbach, Mechanicsville, VA*

PREP: 20 min. + chilling • **COOK:** 20 min. + cooling • **MAKES:** 12 servings (¾ cup each)

4 lbs. medium red potatoes (about 14), peeled and halved
5 hard-boiled large eggs
1 cup chopped dill pickles
1 small onion, chopped
1½ cups mayonnaise
1 tsp. celery seed
½ tsp. salt
¼ tsp. pepper
Paprika

1. Place potatoes in a large saucepan; add water to cover. Bring to a boil. Reduce heat; cook, uncovered, until tender, 15-20 minutes. Drain; cool completely. Cut potatoes into ¾-in. cubes; place in a large bowl.

2. Peel and chop four eggs; peel and slice remaining egg. Add the chopped eggs, pickles and onion to the potatoes. Mix the mayonnaise, celery seed, salt and pepper; stir gently into potato mixture.

3. Top with sliced egg and sprinkle with paprika. Refrigerate, covered, at least 2 hours before serving.

¾ CUP: 326 cal., 22g fat (4g sat. fat), 80mg chol., 413mg sod., 25g carb. (2g sugars, 3g fiber), 6g pro.

✻ READER RAVE

"This is the best potato salad recipe I've ever made! The dill pickles are what make it so delicious. I also tried putting some fresh dill in it, and it turned out great."
—R MBARR059, TASTEOFHOME.COM

FAJITA IN A BOWL

Here's a great summertime game plan: Pull out the skewers and take a stab at grilling peppers, onions and corn for an awesome steak salad.
—*Peggy Woodward, Shullsburg, WI*

TAKES: 30 min. • **MAKES:** 4 servings

1 Tbsp. brown sugar
1 Tbsp. chili powder
½ tsp. salt
1 beef flank steak (1 lb.)
12 miniature sweet peppers, halved and seeded
1 medium red onion, cut into thin wedges
2 cups cherry tomatoes
2 medium ears sweet corn, husks removed

SALAD
12 cups torn mixed salad greens
1 cup fresh cilantro leaves
½ cup reduced-fat lime vinaigrette
Optional ingredients: cotija cheese, lime wedges and tortillas

1. In a small bowl, mix brown sugar, chili powder and salt. Rub onto both sides of steak.

2. Place peppers and onion on a grilling grid; place on grill rack over medium heat. Grill vegetables , covered, 9-11 minutes or until crisp-tender, stirring occasionally; add tomatoes during last 2 minutes. Remove from grill.

3. Place steak and corn directly on grill rack; close lid. Grill steak 8-10 minutes on each side or until a thermometer reads 135° for medium-rare; grill corn for 10-12 minutes or until lightly charred, turning the ears occasionally.

4. Divide greens and cilantro among four bowls. Cut corn from cobs and thinly slice steak across the grain; place in bowls. Top with the vegetables; drizzle with vinaigrette. If desired, serve fajita bowls with cheese, lime and tortillas.

NOTE: If you do not have a grilling grid, use a disposable foil pan with holes poked into the bottom with a meat fork.

1 SERVING: 351 cal., 14g fat (5g sat. fat), 54mg chol., 862mg sod., 33g carb. (16g sugars, 7g fiber), 28g pro.

MOIST PUMPKIN
SCONES, 186

CHAPTER 7

BREADS & ROLLS

What's the coziest, most welcoming smell in the world? Fresh-baked bread, of course! When you make time to bake bread or rolls, you're sending an undeniably delicious message of love.

....

EASY POTATO ROLLS

After I discovered this recipe, it became a mainstay for me. I make the dough ahead of time when company is coming, and I try to keep some in the refrigerator to bake for our ranch hands. Leftover mashed potatoes are almost sure to go into these rolls.
—*Jeanette McKinney, Belleview, MO*

PREP: 20 min. + rising • **BAKE:** 20 min. • **MAKES:** 45 rolls

- 2 pkg. (¼ oz. each) active dry yeast
- 1⅓ cups warm water (110° to 115°), divided
- 1 cup warm mashed potatoes (without added milk and butter)
- ⅔ cup sugar
- ⅔ cup shortening
- 2 large eggs
- 2½ tsp. salt
- 6 to 6½ cups all-purpose flour

❋ READER RAVE

"They are some of the best rolls I've ever tasted! I made one third as dinner rolls and used the rest for cinnamon rolls. Delicious!"

—TERESAFAYES, TASTEOFHOME.COM

1. In a small bowl, dissolve yeast in ⅔ cup warm water. In a large bowl, combine mashed potatoes, sugar, shortening, eggs, salt, remaining ⅔ cup water, yeast mixture and 2 cups flour; beat until smooth. Stir in enough remaining flour to form a soft dough.

2. Do not knead. Shape into a ball; place in a greased bowl, turning once to grease the top. Cover and let rise in a warm place until doubled, about 1 hour.

3. Punch down dough; divide into thirds. Divide and shape one portion into 15 balls; place in a greased 9-in. round baking pan. Cover with a kitchen towel. Repeat with remaining dough. Let rise in a warm place until doubled, about 30 minutes. Preheat oven to 375°.

4. Bake rolls until golden brown, 20-25 minutes. Remove from pans to wire racks. Serve warm.

1 ROLL: 106 cal., 3g fat (1g sat. fat), 8mg chol., 136mg sod., 17g carb. (3g sugars, 1g fiber), 2g pro.

CHOCOLATE ZUCCHINI BREAD

I shred and freeze zucchini from my garden each summer so that I can make this bread all winter long. Our family loves this chocolaty treat.
—*Shari Mckinney, Birney, MT*

PREP: 15 min. • **BAKE:** 50 min. + cooling • **MAKES:** 2 loaves (12 slices each)

2 cups sugar
1 cup canola oil
3 large eggs
3 tsp. vanilla extract
2½ cups all-purpose flour
½ cup baking cocoa
1 tsp. salt
1 tsp. baking soda
1 tsp. ground cinnamon
¼ tsp. baking powder
2 cups shredded peeled zucchini

1. In a large bowl, beat the sugar, oil, eggs and vanilla until well blended. Combine the flour, cocoa, salt, baking soda, cinnamon and baking powder; gradually beat into sugar mixture until blended. Stir in zucchini. Transfer mixture to two 8x4-in. loaf pans coated with cooking spray.

2. Bake at 350° for 50-55 minutes or until a toothpick inserted in the center comes out clean. Cool loaves for 10 minutes before removing from pans to wire racks to cool completely.

1 SLICE: 209 cal., 10g fat (1g sat. fat), 26mg chol., 165mg sod., 28g carb. (17g sugars, 1g fiber), 3g pro.

GARLIC-CHEESE CRESCENT ROLLS

Here's a recipe that just couldn't be much quicker or easier and is sure to add a nice touch to any dinner. The garlic and Parmesan flavors really come through. Enjoy!
—*Lori Abad, East Haven, CT*

TAKES: 20 min. • **MAKES:** 8 servings

1 tube (8 oz.) refrigerated crescent rolls
3 Tbsp. butter, melted
1½ tsp. garlic powder
1 tsp. dried oregano
2 Tbsp. grated Parmesan cheese

1. Preheat oven to 375°. Separate the crescent dough into eight triangles. Roll up from the wide end and place point side down 2 in. apart on an ungreased baking sheet. Curve ends to form a crescent.

2. Combine butter, garlic powder and oregano; brush over rolls. Sprinkle with cheese.

3. Bake rolls for 10-12 minutes or until golden brown. Serve warm.

1 ROLL: 157 cal., 11g fat (4g sat. fat), 12mg chol., 290mg sod., 12g carb. (2g sugars, 0 fiber), 3g pro.

DUTCH APPLE LOAF

Being of Dutch descent, I knew I had to try this recipe. The tender, fruity quick bread freezes well, so I often have a loaf on hand for church bazaars.
—*Gladys Meyer, Ottumwa, IA*

PREP: 15 min. • **BAKE:** 55 min. + cooling • **MAKES:** 1 loaf (16 slices)

½ cup butter, softened
1 cup sugar
2 large eggs
¼ cup buttermilk
1 tsp. vanilla extract
2 cups all-purpose flour
1½ tsp. baking powder
½ tsp. salt
¼ tsp. baking soda
2 cups diced peeled tart apples
½ cup chopped walnuts

TOPPING
¼ cup sugar
¼ cup all-purpose flour
2 tsp. ground cinnamon
¼ cup cold butter, cubed

1. In a large bowl, cream butter and sugar until light and fluffy. Add eggs, one at a time, beating well after each addition. Beat in buttermilk and vanilla. Combine flour, baking powder, salt and baking soda; gradually add to creamed mixture. Fold in apples and walnuts. Pour into a greased 9x5-in. loaf pan.

2. For topping, combine sugar, flour and cinnamon. Cut in butter until mixture resembles coarse crumbs. Sprinkle over batter.

3. Bake at 350° for 55-60 minutes or until a toothpick inserted in the center comes out clean. Cool loaf for 10 minutes before removing from pan to a wire rack.

1 SLICE: 243 cal., 12g fat (6g sat. fat), 50mg chol., 252mg sod., 32g carb. (17g sugars, 1g fiber), 4g pro.

✷ READER RAVE

"This is a wonderful moist apple bread. My family devoured it. I left out the nuts due to allergies. I plan on doubling the recipe and baking it in mini loaf pans to give for Christmas gifts. Thank you for a good, easy recipe."

—CEEGE, TASTEOFHOME.COM

PULL-APART BACON BREAD

I stumbled across this recipe while looking for something different to take to a brunch. Boy, am I glad I did! Everyone asked for the recipe and was surprised it only called for five ingredients. It's the perfect treat to bake for an informal get-together.

—Traci Collins, Cheyenne, WY

PREP: 20 min. + rising • **BAKE:** 55 min. • **MAKES:** 16 servings

12 bacon strips, diced
1 loaf (1 lb.) frozen bread dough, thawed
2 Tbsp. olive oil, divided
1 cup shredded part-skim mozzarella cheese
1 envelope (1 oz.) ranch salad dressing mix

1. In a large skillet, cook bacon over medium heat for 5 minutes or until partially cooked; drain on paper towels. Roll out dough to ½-in. thickness; brush with 1 Tbsp. of oil. Cut dough into 1-in. pieces; place in a large bowl. Add the bacon, cheese, dressing mix and remaining oil; toss to coat.

2. Arrange pieces in a 9x5-in. oval on a parchment paper-lined baking sheet, layering as needed. Cover and let rise in a warm place for 30 minutes or until the dough has doubled.

3. Bake at 350° for 40 minutes. Cover with foil; bake 15 minutes longer or until golden brown.

1 SERVING: 149 cal., 6g fat (2g sat. fat), 8mg chol., 621mg sod., 17g carb. (1g sugars, 1g fiber), 6g pro.

BUTTERY CORNBREAD

A friend gave me this recipe several years ago, and it's my favorite. I love to serve the melt-in-your-mouth cornbread hot from the oven with butter and syrup. It gets rave reviews at family dinners and potlucks alike.
—*Nicole Callen, Auburn, CA*

PREP: 15 min. • **BAKE:** 25 min. • **MAKES:** 15 servings

⅔ cup butter, softened
1 cup sugar
3 large eggs
1⅓ cups 2% milk
2⅓ cups all-purpose flour
1 cup cornmeal
4½ tsp. baking powder
1 tsp. salt

1. Preheat oven to 400°. In a large bowl, cream butter and sugar until light and fluffy. Combine the eggs and milk. Combine flour, cornmeal, baking powder and salt; add to the creamed mixture alternately with the egg mixture.

2. Pour into a greased 13x9-in. baking pan. Bake for 22-27 minutes or until a toothpick inserted in center comes out clean. Cut into squares; serve warm.

1 SERVING: 259 cal., 10g fat (6g sat. fat), 68mg chol., 386mg sod., 37g carb. (15g sugars, 1g fiber), 5g pro.

DOUBLE CORN CORNBREAD: Stir in 1½ cups thawed frozen corn.

MEXICAN CHEESE CORNBREAD: Stir in 1 cup shredded Mexican cheese blend.

JALAPENO CHEESE CORNBREAD: Stir in 1 cup shredded cheddar cheese and 3 finely chopped seeded jalapeno peppers.

MOIST PUMPKIN SCONES

After trying a pumpkin scone at a coffeehouse, I was inspired to look for a recipe to try at home. The glaze nicely complements the pumpkin flavor.
—*Amy McCavour, Gresham, OR*

PREP: 15 min. • **BAKE:** 15 min. + cooling • **MAKES:** 16 scones

4½ cups all-purpose flour
½ cup packed brown sugar
4 tsp. baking powder
3 tsp. pumpkin pie spice
1 tsp. ground cinnamon
½ tsp. baking soda
½ tsp. salt
1 cup cold butter
2 large eggs
1¼ cups canned pumpkin
¾ cup whole milk, divided

GLAZE
2 cups confectioners' sugar
3 Tbsp. whole milk
¼ tsp. pumpkin pie spice

1. In a large bowl, combine the first seven ingredients. Cut in butter until mixture resembles coarse crumbs. In another bowl, whisk the eggs, pumpkin and ½ cup milk. Stir into dry ingredients just until moistened.

2. Turn onto a floured surface; knead 10 times. Divide dough in half. Pat each portion into an 8-in. circle; cut each into eight wedges. Separate wedges and place 1 in. apart on ungreased baking sheets. Brush with the remaining milk.

3. Bake at 400° for 12-15 minutes or until golden brown. Remove to wire racks; cool for 10 minutes. Combine the glaze ingredients; drizzle over scones. Serve warm.

1 SCONE: 338 cal., 13g fat (8g sat. fat), 59mg chol., 348mg sod., 51g carb. (23g sugars, 2g fiber), 5g pro.

SPECIAL BANANA NUT BREAD

This extra-special banana bread makes a wonderful gift for friends and neighbors.
The recipe makes two loaves, so I can serve one right away and keep the
other one in the freezer to use as a last-minute gift.

—Beverly Sprague, Baltimore, MD

....

PREP: 25 min. • **BAKE:** 1 hour + cooling • **MAKES:** 2 loaves (12 slices each)

¾ cup butter, softened
1 pkg. (8 oz.) cream cheese, softened
2 cups sugar
2 large eggs
1½ cups mashed ripe bananas (about 4 medium)
½ tsp. vanilla extract
3 cups all-purpose flour
½ tsp. baking powder
½ tsp. baking soda
½ tsp. salt
2 cups chopped pecans, divided

ORANGE GLAZE
1 cup confectioners' sugar
3 Tbsp. orange juice
1 tsp. grated orange zest

1. Preheat oven to 350°. Cream butter, cream cheese and sugar until light and fluffy. Add eggs, one at a time, beating well after each addition. Beat in bananas and vanilla. In another bowl, combine the flour, baking powder, baking soda and salt; gradually add to the creamed mixture. Fold in 1 cup pecans.

2. Transfer to two greased 8x4-in. loaf pans. Sprinkle with remaining pecans. Bake loaves, covering with foil if they darken too rapidly, until a toothpick inserted in center comes out clean, 1-1¼ hours. Cool 10 minutes before removing to wire racks.

3. While loaves are still slightly warm, whisk glaze ingredients. Drizzle over loaves, using a baking pan or parchment paper under racks to catch the excess. Cool banana bread completely.

1 SLICE: 234 cal., 13g fat (5g sat. fat), 32mg chol., 119mg sod., 29g carb. (18g sugars, 1g fiber), 3g pro.

HAWAIIAN DINNER ROLLS

Pineapple and coconut give a subtle sweetness to these golden homemade rolls. If there are any leftovers, they're great for sandwiches.
—*Kathy Kurtz, Glendora, CA*

PREP: 35 min. + rising • **BAKE:** 15 min. • **MAKES:** 15 rolls

- 1 can (8 oz.) crushed pineapple, undrained
- ¼ cup warm pineapple juice (70° to 80°)
- ¼ cup water (70° to 80°)
- 1 large egg
- ¼ cup butter, cubed
- ¼ cup nonfat dry milk powder
- 1 Tbsp. sugar
- 1½ tsp. salt
- 3¼ cups bread flour
- 2¼ tsp. active dry yeast
- ¾ cup sweetened shredded coconut

1. In bread machine pan, place the first 10 ingredients in order suggested by manufacturer. Select dough setting (check dough after 5 minutes of mixing; add 1-2 Tbsp. of water or flour if needed). Just before final kneading (your machine may audibly signal this), add shredded coconut.

2. When cycle is complete, turn dough onto a lightly floured surface. Cover and let rest for 10 minutes. Divide into 15 portions; roll each into a ball. Place in a greased 13x9-in. baking pan.

3. Cover and let rise in a warm place for 45 minutes or until doubled. Bake at 375° for 15-20 minutes or until golden brown.

NOTE: We recommend you do not use a bread machine's time-delay feature for this recipe.

1 ROLL: 165 cal., 5g fat (3g sat. fat), 23mg chol., 294mg sod., 26g carb. (6g sugars, 1g fiber), 5g pro.

IRISH SODA BREAD

This traditional Irish soda bread can be made with an assortment of mix-ins such as dried fruit and nuts, but I like it with a handful of raisins. It's the perfect change-of-pace item to bring to a party.
—*Gloria Warczak, Cedarburg, WI*

PREP: 15 min. • **BAKE:** 30 min. • **MAKES:** 8 servings

2 cups all-purpose flour
2 Tbsp. brown sugar
1 tsp. baking powder
1 tsp. baking soda
½ tsp. salt
3 Tbsp. cold butter, cubed
2 large eggs, divided use
¾ cup buttermilk
⅓ cup raisins

1. Preheat oven to 375°. Whisk together first five ingredients. Cut in butter until mixture resembles coarse crumbs. In another bowl, whisk together 1 egg and buttermilk. Add to flour mixture; stir just until moistened. Stir in raisins.

2. Turn onto a lightly floured surface; knead gently 6-8 times. Shape into a 6½-in. round loaf; place on a greased baking sheet. Using a sharp knife, make a shallow cross in top of loaf. Whisk remaining egg; brush over top.

3. Bake until golden brown, 30-35 minutes. Remove from pan to a wire rack. Serve warm.

1 SERVING: 210 cal., 6g fat (3g sat. fat), 59mg chol., 463mg sod., 33g carb. (8g sugars, 1g fiber), 6g pro.

CARAWAY IRISH SODA BREAD: Add 1-2 Tbsp. caraway seeds to the dry ingredients.

MOM'S ITALIAN BREAD

I think Mom used to bake at least four of these tender loaves at once, and they never lasted long. She served the bread with every Italian meal. I love it toasted, too.

—*Linda Harrington, Windham, NH*

PREP: 30 min. + rising • **BAKE:** 20 min. + cooling • **MAKES:** 2 loaves (12 slices each)

- 1 pkg. (¼ oz.) active dry yeast
- 2 cups warm water (110° to 115°)
- 1 tsp. sugar
- 2 tsp. salt
- 5½ cups all-purpose flour

✱ TEST KITCHEN TIP

To ensure a light texture, take time to knead the dough well. After the first few minutes of kneading, gently press your thumb into the dough. If the indentation stays, you're finished kneading. If not, continue kneading a few minutes longer.

1. In a large bowl, dissolve yeast in warm water. Add sugar, salt and 3 cups flour. Beat on medium speed for 3 minutes. Stir in remaining flour to form a soft dough.

2. Turn onto a floured surface; knead until smooth and elastic, about 6-8 minutes. Place in a greased bowl, turning once to grease the top. Cover and let rise in a warm place until doubled, about 1 hour.

3. Punch dough down. Turn onto a floured surface; divide in half. Shape each portion into a loaf. Place each loaf seam side down on a greased baking sheet. Cover and let rise until doubled, about 30 minutes.

4. Meanwhile, preheat oven to 400°. With a sharp knife, make four shallow slashes across top of each loaf. Bake 20-25 minutes or until golden brown. Remove from pans to wire racks to cool.

1 SLICE: 106 cal., 0 fat (0 sat. fat), 0 chol., 197mg sod., 22g carb. (1g sugars, 1g fiber), 3g pro. *Diabetic exchanges:* 1½ starch.

MAKE-AHEAD BUTTERHORNS

Mom loved to make these lightly sweet, golden rolls. They're beautiful and impressive to serve, and they have a wonderful taste that carries with it the best memories of home.
—*Bernice Morris, Marshfield, MO*

PREP: 30 min. + freezing • **BAKE:** 15 min. • **MAKES:** 32 rolls

2 pkg. (¼ oz. each) active dry yeast
⅓ cup warm water (110° to 115°)
2 cups warm 2% milk (110° to 115°)
1 cup shortening
1 cup sugar
6 large eggs
2 tsp. salt
9 cups all-purpose flour, divided
3 to 4 Tbsp. butter, melted

1. Preheat oven to 375°. In a large bowl, dissolve yeast in water. Add milk, shortening, sugar, eggs, salt and 4 cups flour; beat 3 minutes or until smooth. Add enough remaining flour to form a soft dough.

2. Turn onto a floured surface; knead lightly. Place in a greased bowl, turning once to grease top. Cover and let rise in a warm place until doubled, about 2 hours.

3. Punch dough down; divide into four equal parts. Roll each into a 9-in. circle; brush with butter. Cut each circle into eight pie-shaped wedges; roll up each wedge from wide edge to tip of dough and pinch dough to seal.

4. Place rolls with tip down on baking sheets; freeze. When frozen, place in freezer bags and seal. Store in freezer for up to 4 weeks.

5. Place on greased baking sheets; thaw 5 hours or until doubled in size. Bake 12-15 minutes or until lightly browned. Remove from baking sheets; serve warm, or cool on wire rack.

1 ROLL: 239 cal., 9g fat (3g sat. fat), 39mg chol., 178mg sod., 34g carb. (7g sugars, 1g fiber), 6g pro.

**LUSCIOUS ALMOND
CHEESECAKE, 220**

CAKES, PIES & MORE

A pretty dessert to share makes any occasion a cause to celebrate. In this chapter, you'll find lovely cakes, pretty pies, luscious cheesecakes and more.

JUICY CHERRY PIE

Tart cherry season comes in the heart of summer. Choose fresh tart cherries that are bright colored, shiny, plump and relatively firm when pressed lightly.
—*Karen Berner, New Canaan, CT*

PREP: 35 min. + chilling • **BAKE:** 55 min. + cooling • **MAKES:** 8 servings

2½ cups all-purpose flour
½ tsp. salt
⅔ cup cold unsalted butter, cubed
⅓ cup shortening
6 to 10 Tbsp. ice water

FILLING
5 cups fresh tart cherries, pitted
2 tsp. lemon juice
¼ tsp. almond extract
1 cup sugar
⅓ cup all-purpose flour
1 tsp. ground cinnamon

SUGAR TOPPING
1 Tbsp. 2% milk
1 tsp. sugar

1. In a large bowl, mix flour and salt; cut in butter and shortening until crumbly. Gradually add ice water, tossing with a fork until dough holds together when pressed. Divide dough in half. Shape each into a disk; wrap in plastic. Refrigerate 1 hour or overnight.

2. Preheat oven to 375°. For the filling, place cherries in a large bowl; drizzle with lemon juice and almond extract. In a small bowl, mix sugar, flour and cinnamon. Sprinkle over cherries and toss gently to coat.

3. On a lightly floured surface, roll one half of dough to a ⅛-in.-thick circle; transfer to a 9-in. pie plate. Trim the pastry even with rim. Add filling.

4. Roll remaining dough to a ⅛-in.-thick circle; cut out stars or other shapes using cookie cutters. Place top pastry over filling. Trim, seal and flute edge. If desired, decorate top with cutouts.

5. Bake 40 minutes. For topping, brush top of pie with milk; sprinkle with sugar. Bake 15-20 minutes longer or until crust is golden brown and filling is bubbly. Cool on a wire rack.

1 PIECE: 521 cal., 24g fat (12g sat. fat), 41mg chol., 155mg sod., 72g carb. (34g sugars, 3g fiber), 6g pro.

PINEAPPLE SHEET CAKE

This sheet cake is perfect for serving a crowd. It keeps so well that you can easily prepare it a day ahead and be assured it will stay moist. I often bring it to church potlucks, and I have yet to take much of it home.

—*Kim Miller Spiek, Sarasota, FL*

PREP: 15 min. • **BAKE:** 35 min. + cooling • **MAKES:** about 24 servings

CAKE
- 2 cups all-purpose flour
- 2 cups sugar
- 2 large eggs
- 1 cup chopped nuts
- 2 tsp. baking soda
- ½ tsp. salt
- 1 tsp. vanilla extract
- 1 can (20 oz.) crushed pineapple, undrained

CREAM CHEESE ICING
- 1 pkg. (8 oz.) cream cheese, softened
- ½ cup butter, softened
- 3¾ cups confectioners' sugar
- 1 tsp. vanilla extract
- ½ cup chopped nuts

1. In a large bowl, combine cake ingredients; beat until smooth. Pour into a greased 15x10x1-in. baking pan. Bake at 350° for 35 minutes. Cool.

2. For icing, in a small bowl, combine cream cheese, butter, confectioners' sugar and vanilla until smooth. Spread over cake and sprinkle with nuts.

1 PIECE: 315 cal., 12g fat (5g sat. fat), 38mg chol., 227mg sod., 49g carb. (39g sugars, 1g fiber), 4g pro.

✳ TEST KITCHEN TIP
Don't worry if the top of this cake looks dark; it's not overbaked. Cakes with large amounts of baking soda in them tend to darken because the soda is a browning agent.

GRANDMA'S RED VELVET CAKE

No one believes it's Christmas at our house until this jolly cake appears. It's different from other red velvets I've tasted; the icing is as light as snow.

—*Kathryn Davison, Charlotte, NC*

PREP: 30 min. • **BAKE:** 20 min. + cooling • **MAKES:** 14 servings

½ cup butter, softened
1½ cups sugar
2 large eggs
2 bottles (1 oz. each) red food coloring
1 Tbsp. white vinegar
1 tsp. vanilla extract
2¼ cups cake flour
2 Tbsp. baking cocoa
1 tsp. baking soda
1 tsp. salt
1 cup buttermilk

FROSTING
1 Tbsp. cornstarch
½ cup cold water
2 cups butter, softened
2 tsp. vanilla extract
3½ cups confectioners' sugar

1. Preheat oven to 350°. Cream the butter and sugar until light and fluffy. Add eggs, one at a time, beating well after each addition. Beat in food coloring, vinegar and vanilla. In another bowl, whisk together flour, cocoa, baking soda and salt; add to the creamed mixture alternately with the buttermilk, beating well after each addition.

2. Pour into two greased and floured 9-in. round baking pans. Bake until a toothpick inserted in the center comes out clean, 20-25 minutes. Cool layers 10 minutes before removing from pans to wire racks to cool completely.

3. For frosting, combine water and cornstarch in a small saucepan over medium heat. Stir until thickened and opaque, 2-3 minutes. Cool to room temperature. Beat butter and vanilla until light and fluffy. Beat in cornstarch mixture. Gradually add the confectioners' sugar; beat until light and fluffy. Spread the frosting between layers and over top and sides of cake.

1 SLICE: 595 cal., 34g fat (21g sat. fat), 115mg chol., 564mg sod., 71g carb. (52g sugars, 1g fiber), 4g pro.

PEANUT BUTTER BROWNIE TRIFLE

This rich, tempting trifle feeds a crowd and features the ever-popular combination of chocolate and peanut butter. Try this dessert for your next get-together.
—*Nancy Foust, Stoneboro, PA*

PREP: 1 hour + chilling • **MAKES:** 20 servings (1 cup each)

- 1 fudge brownie mix (13x9-in. pan size)
- 1 pkg. (10 oz.) peanut butter chips
- 2 pkg. (13 oz. each) miniature peanut butter cups
- 4 cups cold 2% milk
- 2 pkg. (5.1 oz. each) instant vanilla pudding mix
- 1 cup creamy peanut butter
- 4 tsp. vanilla extract
- 3 cartons (8 oz. each) frozen whipped topping, thawed

1. Preheat oven to 350°. Prepare brownie batter according to package directions; stir in peanut butter chips. Bake in a greased 13x9-in. baking pan for 20-25 minutes or until a toothpick inserted in center comes out with moist crumbs (do not overbake). Cool on a wire rack; cut into ¾-in. pieces.

2. Cut peanut butter cups in half; set aside ⅓ cup for garnish. In a large bowl, whisk milk and pudding mixes for 2 minutes (mixture will be thick). Add the peanut butter and vanilla; mix well. Fold in 1½ cartons of the whipped topping.

3. Place a third of the brownies in a 5-qt. glass bowl; top with a third of the remaining peanut butter cups. Spoon a third of the pudding mixture over the top. Repeat layers twice. Cover with remaining whipped topping; garnish with reserved peanut butter cups. Refrigerate until chilled.

1 CUP: 680 cal., 38g fat (15g sat. fat), 28mg chol., 547mg sod., 73g carb. (54g sugars, 3g fiber), 13g pro.

JUMBLEBERRY CRUMBLE

A friend brought this down-home dessert to church and was kind enough to give out the recipe. Everyone enjoyed it so much and showered her with compliments. It's especially wonderful served warm with ice cream or a dollop of creamy whipped topping.

—*Mary Ann Dell, Phoenixville, PA*

PREP: 10 min. + standing • **BAKE:** 45 min. • **MAKES:** 8 servings

- 3 cups halved fresh strawberries
- 1½ cups fresh raspberries
- 1½ cups fresh blueberries
- ⅔ cup sugar
- 3 Tbsp. quick-cooking tapioca
- ½ cup all-purpose flour
- ½ cup quick-cooking oats
- ½ cup packed brown sugar
- 1 tsp. ground cinnamon
- ⅓ cup butter, melted
- Vanilla ice cream or sweetened whipped cream, optional

1. In a large bowl, combine strawberries, raspberries and blueberries. Combine sugar and tapioca; sprinkle over berries and toss gently. Pour the mixture into a greased 11x7-in. baking dish; let stand for 15 minutes.

2. Meanwhile, in a small bowl, combine the flour, oats, brown sugar and cinnamon. Stir in butter; sprinkle over berry mixture.

3. Bake at 350° for 45-50 minutes or until filling is bubbly and topping is golden brown. Serve warm and, if desired, with vanilla ice cream or sweetened whipped cream.

1 SERVING: 290 cal., 8g fat (5g sat. fat), 20mg chol., 84mg sod., 54g carb. (36g sugars, 4g fiber), 2g pro.

CAST-IRON PEACH CROSTATA

While the crostata, an open-faced fruit tart, is actually Italian,
my version's peach filling is American all the way.
—*Lauren Knoelke, Des Moines, IA*

PREP: 45 min. + chilling • **BAKE:** 45 min. • **MAKES:** 10 servings

1½ cups all-purpose flour
2 Tbsp. plus ¾ cup packed brown sugar, divided
1¼ tsp. salt, divided
½ cup cold unsalted butter, cubed
2 Tbsp. shortening
3 to 5 Tbsp. ice water
8 cups sliced peaches (about 7-8 medium)
1 Tbsp. lemon juice
3 Tbsp. cornstarch
½ tsp. ground cinnamon
¼ tsp. ground nutmeg
1 large egg, beaten
2 Tbsp. sliced almonds
1 Tbsp. coarse sugar
⅓ cup water
1 cup fresh raspberries, optional

1. Mix flour, 2 Tbsp. brown sugar and 1 tsp. salt; cut in butter and shortening until crumbly. Gradually add ice water, tossing with a fork until dough holds together when pressed. Shape dough into a disk; wrap in plastic. Refrigerate 1 hour or overnight.

2. Combine peaches and lemon juice. Add remaining brown sugar, cornstarch, spices and remaining salt; toss gently. Let stand 30 minutes.

3. Preheat oven to 400°. On a lightly floured surface, roll dough into a 13-in. circle; transfer to a 10-in. cast-iron skillet, letting excess hang over edge. Using a slotted spoon, transfer peaches into pastry, reserving liquid. Fold pastry edge over filling, pleating as you go, leaving center uncovered. Brush folded pastry with beaten egg; sprinkle with almonds and coarse sugar. Bake until crust is dark golden and filling is bubbly, 45-55 minutes.

4. In a small saucepan, combine reserved liquid and water; bring to a boil. Simmer until thickened, 1-2 minutes; serve warm with pie. If desired, top with fresh raspberries.

1 SLICE: 322 cal., 13g fat (7g sat. fat), 43mg chol., 381mg sod., 49g carb. (30g sugars, 3g fiber), 4g pro.

CHOCOLATE CHEESECAKE

Everyone's a chocolate lover when it comes to this special dessert. "It melts in your mouth...very smooth and fudgy" are typical comments guests make after they take a bite. For a fun taste twist, spoon cherry or strawberry topping over each slice.

—*Sue Call, Beech Grove, IN*

PREP: 20 min. • **BAKE:** 40 min. + chilling • **MAKES:** 12 servings

1 cup crushed chocolate wafer crumbs
3 Tbsp. sugar
3 Tbsp. butter, melted

FILLING

2 cups (12 oz.) semisweet chocolate chips
2 pkg. (8 oz. each) cream cheese, softened
¾ cup sugar
2 Tbsp. all-purpose flour
2 large eggs, lightly beaten
1 tsp. vanilla extract
Strawberries and white chocolate shavings, optional

1. In a small bowl, combine cookie crumbs and sugar; stir in butter. Press onto the bottom of a greased 9-in. springform pan; set aside. In a microwave, melt the chocolate chips; stir until smooth. Set aside.

2. In a large bowl, beat the cream cheese, sugar and flour until smooth. Add eggs; beat on low just until combined. Stir in vanilla and melted chocolate just until blended. Pour filling over crust.

3. Bake at 350° for 40-45 minutes or until center is almost set. Cool cake on a wire rack for 10 minutes. Carefully run a knife around edge of pan to loosen; cool 1 hour longer. Refrigerate overnight.

4. If desired, garnish slices with strawberries and chocolate shavings. Refrigerate leftovers.

1 SLICE: 411 cal., 26g fat (15g sat. fat), 77mg chol., 211mg sod., 44g carb. (36g sugars, 2g fiber), 5g pro.

ORANGE BUTTERMILK CUPCAKES

Simple and delicious, this is our all-time favorite light dessert.
You'll be surprised how well the citrus flavor comes through in every bite.
—*Kim Chester, Cartersville, GA*

PREP: 20 min. • **BAKE:** 20 min. + cooling • **MAKES:** 9 servings

3 Tbsp. butter, softened
⅓ cup packed brown sugar
¼ cup sugar blend
1 tsp. grated orange zest
1 large egg
1 large egg white
2 Tbsp. plus 2½ tsp. orange juice, divided
1¼ cups cake flour
¾ tsp. baking powder
¼ tsp. baking soda
¼ tsp. salt
¼ tsp. ground ginger
⅔ cup buttermilk
½ cup confectioners' sugar

1. In a large bowl, beat the butter, brown sugar, sugar blend and orange zest. Beat in the egg, egg white and 2 Tbsp. orange juice. Combine flour, baking powder, baking soda, salt and ginger; gradually add to the butter mixture alternately with buttermilk, beating well after each addition.

2. Coat nine muffin cups with cooking spray or use paper liners; fill three-fourths full with batter. Bake at 350° for 18-20 minutes or until a toothpick inserted in the center comes out clean. Cool for 5 minutes before removing from pan to a wire rack to cool completely.

3. In a small bowl, combine confectioners' sugar and remaining orange juice. Frost cupcakes.

NOTE: This recipe was tested with Splenda sugar blend.

1 CUPCAKE: 201 cal., 5g fat (3g sat. fat), 35mg chol., 208mg sod., 37g carb. (21g sugars, 0 fiber), 3g pro.

MOIST PUMPKIN TUBE CAKE

This cake is perfect for fall. As it bakes, the spicy aroma fills the house.
—*Virginia Loew, Leesburg, FL*

PREP: 10 min. • **BAKE:** 1 hour + cooling • **MAKES:** 16 servings

2½ cups sugar
1 cup canola oil
3 large eggs
3 cups all-purpose flour
2 tsp. baking soda
1 tsp. ground cinnamon
1 tsp. ground nutmeg
½ tsp. salt
¼ tsp. ground cloves
1 can (15 oz.) solid-pack pumpkin
   Confectioners' sugar

1. Preheat oven to 350°. In a large bowl, combine sugar and oil until blended. Add eggs, one at a time, beating well after each addition. Combine the flour, baking soda, cinnamon, nutmeg, salt and cloves; add to egg mixture alternately with pumpkin, beating well after each addition.

2. Transfer to a greased 10-in. fluted tube pan. Bake 60-65 minutes or until toothpick inserted in the center comes out clean. Cool 10 minutes before inverting onto a wire rack. Remove pan and cool completely. Dust with confectioners' sugar.

1 SLICE: 351 cal., 15g fat (2g sat. fat), 40mg chol., 245mg sod., 51g carb. (32g sugars, 2g fiber), 4g pro.

✱ DID YOU KNOW?

Most of the world's canned pumpkin is produced in a Libby's factory in Morton, located near Peoria in central Illinois. Local farmers plant about 5,000 acres of pumpkin per year.

CHOCOLATE MALT PUDDING CAKE

When I make this amazing cake, I chop the malted milk balls by putting them in a plastic bag and pounding it with a rubber mallet. It completely eliminates the mess.
—*Sarah Skubinna, Cascade, MT*

PREP: 25 min. • **COOK:** 2 hours + standing • **MAKES:** 8 servings

½ cup 2% milk
2 Tbsp. canola oil
½ tsp. almond extract
1 cup all-purpose flour
½ cup packed brown sugar
2 Tbsp. baking cocoa
1½ tsp. baking powder
½ cup coarsely chopped malted milk balls
½ cup semisweet chocolate chips
¾ cup sugar
¼ cup malted milk powder
1¼ cups boiling water
4 oz. cream cheese, softened and cubed
Vanilla ice cream and sliced almonds, optional

1. In a large bowl, combine milk, oil and extract. Combine flour, brown sugar, cocoa and baking powder; gradually beat into milk mixture until blended. Stir in milk balls and chocolate chips.

2. Spoon into a greased 3-qt. slow cooker. In a small bowl, combine sugar and milk powder; stir in water and cream cheese. Pour over batter (do not stir).

3. Cover and cook on high for 2-3 hours or until a toothpick inserted in center of cake comes out clean. Turn off heat. Let stand 15 minutes. Serve warm, with ice cream and sprinkled almonds if desired.

1 SERVING: 430 cal., 17g fat (8g sat. fat), 19mg chol., 167mg sod., 67g carb. (50g sugars, 2g fiber), 6g pro.

LUSCIOUS ALMOND CHEESECAKE

Almonds and almond extract give an elegant and tasty twist
to a traditional sour cream-topped cheesecake.
—*Brenda Clifford, Overland Park, KS*

PREP: 15 min. • **BAKE:** 55 min. + chilling • **MAKES:** 16 servings

1¼ cups crushed vanilla
   wafers (about 40)
¾ cup finely chopped
   almonds
¼ cup sugar
⅓ cup butter, melted

FILLING
4 pkg. (8 oz. each) cream
   cheese, softened
1¼ cups sugar
4 large eggs, lightly
   beaten
1½ tsp. almond extract
1 tsp. vanilla extract

TOPPING
2 cups sour cream
¼ cup sugar
1 tsp. vanilla extract
⅛ cup toasted sliced
   almonds

1. In a bowl, combine the wafer crumbs, almonds and sugar; stir in the butter and mix well. Press into the bottom of a greased 10-in. springform pan; set aside.

2. In a large bowl, beat the cream cheese and sugar until smooth. Add the eggs; beat on low speed just until combined. Stir in extracts. Pour into crust. Place on a baking sheet.

3. Bake at 350° for 50-55 minutes or until center is almost set. Remove from the oven; let stand for 5 minutes (leave oven on). Combine the sour cream, sugar and vanilla. Spoon around edge of cheesecake; carefully spread over filling. Bake 5 minutes longer. Cool on a wire rack for 10 minutes. Carefully run a knife around edge of pan to loosen; cool cake 1 hour longer. Refrigerate overnight.

4. Just before serving, sprinkle with almonds and remove sides of pan. Refrigerate leftovers.

1 SLICE: 329 cal., 20g fat (10g sat. fat), 100mg chol., 140mg sod., 32g carb. (26g sugars, 1g fiber), 5g pro.

SWEDISH APPLE PIE

This decadent-tasting but lighter apple pie serves up homemade flavor in every bite. It's a perfect snack with coffee or as an after-dinner treat.
—*Sarah Klier, Ada, MI*

PREP: 15 min. • **BAKE:** 25 min. • **MAKES:** 8 servings

½ cup sugar
¼ cup whole wheat flour
¼ cup all-purpose flour
1 tsp. baking powder
½ tsp. salt
½ tsp. ground cinnamon
1 large egg
¼ tsp. vanilla extract
2 medium tart apples, chopped
¾ cup chopped walnuts or pecans, toasted
Confectioners' sugar, optional

1. In a large bowl, combine the sugar, flours, baking powder, salt and cinnamon. In a small bowl, whisk the egg and vanilla. Stir into the dry ingredients just until moistened. Fold in apples and walnuts.

2. Transfer to a 9-in. pie plate coated with cooking spray. Bake pie at 350° for 25-30 minutes or until a toothpick inserted in the center comes out clean. Sprinkle with confectioners' sugar if desired. Serve pie warm.

1 PIECE: 174 cal., 7g fat (1g sat. fat), 26mg chol., 207mg sod., 25g carb. (16g sugars, 2g fiber), 5g pro. *Diabetic exchanges:* 1½ starch, 1 fat.

✱ DID YOU KNOW?

Swedish apple pie is a snap to make because it doesn't have a crust like traditional pies.

CALIFORNIA LEMON POUND CAKE

Citrus trees grow abundantly in California, and I'm always looking for new recipes that use fruit from the orange and lemon trees in my yard. This is one of my favorites, a beloved recipe my mother passed down to me.
—*Richard Killeaney, Spring Valley, CA*

PREP: 15 min. • **BAKE:** 70 min. + cooling • **MAKES:** 16 servings

1   cup butter, softened
½   cup shortening
3   cups sugar
5   large eggs
1   Tbsp. grated lemon zest
1   Tbsp. lemon extract
3   cups all-purpose flour
1   tsp. salt
½   tsp. baking powder
1   cup whole milk

FROSTING

¼   cup butter, softened
1¾ cups confectioners' sugar
2   Tbsp. lemon juice
1   tsp. grated lemon zest

1. In a large bowl, cream the butter, shortening and sugar until light and fluffy, about 5 minutes. Add eggs, one at a time, beating well after each addition. Stir in lemon zest and extract. Combine the flour, salt and baking powder; gradually add to creamed mixture alternately with milk. Beat just until combined.

2. Pour into a greased 10-in. fluted tube pan. Bake at 350° for 70 minutes or until a toothpick inserted in the center comes out clean. Cool for 10 minutes before removing from pan to a wire rack to cool completely.

3. In a small bowl, combine the frosting ingredients; beat until smooth. Spread over top of cake.

1 SLICE: 500 cal., 23g fat (11g sat. fat), 107mg chol., 333mg sod., 70g carb. (50g sugars, 1g fiber), 5g pro.

✳ TEST KITCHEN TIP

For extra nonstick insurance, grease the cake pan with shortening, then give the greased pan a quick spritz of cooking spray. A flexible plastic knife works wonders to remove a cake from a fluted tube pan without damage. Slide the knife along the sides and center of the pan to loosen the cake before inverting it.

**FROSTED FUDGE
BROWNIES, 252**

CHAPTER 9

COOKIES, BARS & BROWNIES

Cute, fun, portable, and ready to give, send or share...cookies always bring smiles by the dozen! Discover our best-loved brownies and bars, too.

FROSTED CRANBERRY DROP COOKIES

I started making these treats after tasting a batch my friend whipped up. I immediately requested the recipe and have been baking them by the dozens ever since. The sweet icing beautifully complements the tart berries.
—*Shirley Kidd, New London, MN*

PREP: 25 min. • **BAKE:** 15 min./batch + cooling • **MAKES:** about 5 dozen

½ cup butter, softened
1   cup sugar
¾ cup packed brown sugar
¼ cup whole milk
1   large egg
2   Tbsp. orange juice
3   cups all-purpose flour
1   tsp. baking powder
½ tsp. salt
¼ tsp. baking soda
2½ cups chopped fresh or frozen cranberries
1   cup chopped walnuts

FROSTING
⅓ cup butter
2   cups confectioners' sugar
1½ tsp. vanilla extract
2   to 4 Tbsp. hot water

1. In a bowl, cream butter and sugars. Add milk, egg and orange juice; mix well. Combine the flour, baking powder, salt and baking soda; add to the creamed mixture and mix well. Stir in cranberries and nuts.

2. Drop by tablespoonfuls 2 in. apart onto greased baking sheets. Bake at 350° until golden brown, 12-15 minutes. Cool on wire racks.

3. For frosting, heat the butter in a saucepan over low heat until golden brown, about 5 minutes. Cool for 2 minutes; transfer to a small bowl. Add sugar and vanilla. Beat in water, 1 Tbsp. at a time, until frosting reaches desired consistency. Frost the cookies.

1 COOKIE: 102 cal., 4g fat (2g sat. fat), 10mg chol., 56mg sod., 16g carb. (10g sugars, 0 fiber), 1g pro.

WHITE VELVET CUTOUTS

We make and decorate these cutouts for different holidays, and we give lots of them as gifts. Last year, we baked a batch a week before Christmas to be sure we'd have plenty to give and plenty for ourselves, too. These rich cookies melt in your mouth.

—*Kim Hinkle, Wauseon, OH*

PREP: 25 min. + chilling • **BAKE:** 10 min./batch + cooling • **MAKES:** about 5½ dozen

2 cups butter, softened
1 pkg. (8 oz.) cream cheese, softened
2 cups sugar
2 large egg yolks
1 tsp. vanilla extract
4½ cups all-purpose flour

FROSTING
3 Tbsp. butter, softened
1 Tbsp. shortening
½ tsp. vanilla extract
3½ cups confectioners' sugar
4 to 5 Tbsp. 2% milk
Food coloring, optional

1. In a large bowl, cream butter, cream cheese and sugar until light and fluffy. Beat in egg yolks and vanilla. Gradually beat flour into creamed mixture. Divide dough in half. Shape each into a disk; wrap and refrigerate 2 hours or until firm enough to roll.

2. Preheat oven to 350°. On a lightly floured surface, roll each portion of dough to ¼-in. thickness. Cut with floured 3-in. cookie cutters. Place 1 in. apart on greased baking sheets. Bake 10-12 minutes or until set (do not brown). Cool on pans 5 minutes. Remove to wire racks to cool completely.

3. For frosting, in a bowl, beat butter, shortening and vanilla until blended. Beat in confectioners' sugar and enough milk to reach spreading consistency; beat for 3 minutes or until light and fluffy. If desired, beat in food coloring. Frost cookies. (Keep frosting covered with a damp towel to prevent it from drying out.)

1 COOKIE: 149 cal., 8g fat (5g sat. fat), 26mg chol., 62mg sod., 19g carb. (13g sugars, 0 fiber), 1g pro.

MOUNTAIN COOKIES

I've been making these deliciously different cookies for over 10 years. My kids especially like the creamy coconut filling. Wherever I take a batch to share, people ask for the recipe. You'll be hard-pressed to eat just one!

—*Jeanne Adams, Richmond, VT*

PREP: 30 min. • **BAKE:** 10 min. • **MAKES:** 4 dozen

1 cup butter, softened
1 cup confectioners' sugar
2 tsp. vanilla extract
2 cups all-purpose flour
½ tsp. salt

FILLING
3 oz. cream cheese, softened
1 cup confectioners' sugar
2 Tbsp. all-purpose flour
1 tsp. vanilla extract
½ cup finely chopped pecans
½ cup sweetened shredded coconut

TOPPING
½ cup semisweet chocolate chips
2 Tbsp. butter
2 Tbsp. water
½ cup confectioners' sugar

1. In a large bowl, cream butter and sugar until light and fluffy. Beat in vanilla. Combine flour and salt; gradually add to the creamed mixture and mix well.

2. Shape into 1-in. balls; place 2 in. apart on ungreased baking sheets. Make a deep indentation in the center of each cookie. Bake at 350° until the edges just start to brown, 10-12 minutes. Remove to wire racks to cool completely.

3. For the filling, in a large bowl, beat the cream cheese, sugar, flour and vanilla until smooth. Add pecans and coconut. Spoon ½ tsp. into each cookie.

4. For topping, in a microwave-safe bowl, melt chocolate chips and butter with water; stir until smooth. Stir in sugar. Drizzle over cookies.

1 COOKIE: 111 cal., 7g fat (4g sat. fat), 13mg chol., 67mg sod., 12g carb. (8g sugars, 0 fiber), 1g pro.

CANNOLI WAFER SANDWICHES

My family loves to visit a local Italian restaurant that has a wonderful dessert buffet. The cannoli are among our favorites, so I just had to come up with my own simple version. These are best served the same day so the wafers stay nice and crisp.

—Nichi Larson, Shawnee, KS

PREP: 35 min. + standing • **MAKES:** 3½ dozen

1 cup whole-milk ricotta cheese
¼ cup confectioners' sugar
1 Tbsp. sugar
¼ tsp. vanilla extract
1 pkg. (12 oz.) vanilla wafers
12 oz. white candy coating, melted
½ cup miniature semisweet chocolate chips
 Additional confectioners' sugar

1. In a small bowl, mix ricotta cheese, confectioners' sugar, sugar and vanilla until blended. Spread 1 scant tsp. filling on bottoms of half of the wafers; cover with remaining wafers.

2. Dip each sandwich cookie halfway into candy coating; allow excess to drip off. Place on waxed paper; sprinkle with chocolate chips. Let stand until set, about 10 minutes.

3. Serve within 2 hours or refrigerate until serving. Dust with additional confectioners' sugar just before serving.

1 COOKIE: 93 cal., 5g fat (3g sat. fat), 4mg chol., 38mg sod., 13g carb. (10g sugars, 0 fiber), 1g pro.

＊ TEST KITCHEN TIP

To create a classically flavored variation, add a little finely grated orange zest to the filling. And instead of mini chips, sprinkle the cookies with finely chopped pistachios.

COFFEE & CREAM BROWNIES

A friend gave me the recipe for these cakelike brownies topped with creamy coffee filling and a chocolate glaze. I like to garnish each square with a chocolate-covered coffee bean.

—*Michelle Tiemstra, Lacombe, AB*

PREP: 35 min. • **BAKE:** 25 min. + standing • **MAKES:** 16 servings

½ cup butter, cubed
3 oz. unsweetened chocolate, chopped
2 large eggs
1 cup sugar
1 tsp. vanilla extract
⅔ cup all-purpose flour
¼ tsp. baking soda

FILLING
1 tsp. instant coffee granules
3 Tbsp. heavy whipping cream
1 cup confectioners' sugar
2 Tbsp. butter, softened

GLAZE
1 cup (6 oz.) semisweet chocolate chips
⅓ cup heavy whipping cream

1. In a microwave, melt butter and chocolate; stir until smooth. Cool slightly. In a small bowl, beat the eggs, sugar and vanilla; stir in chocolate mixture. Combine flour and baking soda; stir into chocolate mixture.

2. Spread into a greased 8-in. square baking pan. Bake at 350° for 25-30 minutes or until a toothpick inserted in center comes out clean (do not overbake). Cool on a wire rack.

3. For filling, dissolve coffee granules in cream. Add confectioners' sugar and butter; beat just until light and fluffy (do not overbeat). Spread over brownies. Refrigerate until set.

4. In a small saucepan, combine chips and cream. Cook and stir over low heat until the chips are melted. Cool slightly. Carefully spread over the filling. Let stand for 30 minutes or until glaze is set. Cut into squares. Store in the refrigerator.

1 BROWNIE: 282 cal., 17g fat (10g sat. fat), 51mg chol., 91mg sod., 33g carb. (26g sugars, 2g fiber), 3g pro.

COCONUT CLOUDS

The big dollop of buttercream and a sprinkle of roasty-toasty coconut make these soft cookies the first to disappear from Christmas cookie trays. Take care to toast the coconut for absolutely heavenly flavor.
—*Donna Scofield, Yakima, WA*

PREP: 45 min. • **BAKE:** 10 min./batch + cooling • **MAKES:** about 5½ dozen

¼ cup butter, softened
¼ cup shortening
1 cup sugar
½ cup packed brown sugar
2 large eggs
1 tsp. coconut extract
1 tsp. vanilla extract
1 cup sour cream
2¾ cups all-purpose flour
1 tsp. salt
½ tsp. baking soda
1 cup sweetened shredded coconut, toasted

BROWNED BUTTER FROSTING

⅓ cup butter, cubed
3 cups confectioners' sugar
3 Tbsp. evaporated milk
1 tsp. coconut extract
1 tsp. vanilla extract
2 cups sweetened shredded coconut, toasted

1. Preheat oven to 375°. Cream butter, shortening and sugars until light and fluffy; beat in eggs and extracts. Stir in the sour cream. In another bowl, whisk together flour, salt and baking soda; gradually beat into the creamed mixture. Stir in coconut.

2. Drop the dough by tablespoonfuls 2 in. apart onto lightly greased baking sheets. Bake cookies until set, 8-10 minutes. Remove to wire racks to cool completely.

3. In a small heavy saucepan, heat butter over medium heat until golden brown, about 5-7 minutes, stirring constantly. Transfer to a small bowl; gradually beat in confectioners' sugar, milk and extracts. Spread over cookies. Dip in coconut; let stand until set. Store in an airtight container.

NOTE: To toast coconut, bake in a shallow pan in a 350° oven for 5-10 minutes or cook in a skillet over low heat until golden brown, stirring occasionally.

1 COOKIE: 110 cal., 5g fat (3g sat. fat), 13mg chol., 72mg sod., 16g carb. (11g sugars, 0 fiber), 1g pro.

CHOCOLATE COVERED CHERRY THUMBPRINTS

When I dig out my best cookie recipes, they remind me of baking when my children were little. These thumbprints with cherries elicit sweet memories.
—*Deborah Puette, Lilburn, GA*

....

PREP: 30 min. + chilling • **BAKE:** 15 min. + cooling • **MAKES:** 2 dozen

¼   cup butter, softened
¼   cup shortening
¼   cup packed brown sugar
¼   tsp. salt
1   large egg, separated
½   tsp. vanilla extract
1   cup all-purpose flour
1   cup finely chopped salted roasted almonds

FILLING
⅓   cup confectioners' sugar
1   Tbsp. maraschino cherry juice
2   tsp. butter, softened
1   tsp. 2% milk

TOPPINGS
24 maraschino cherries
4   oz. milk chocolate candy coating, melted

1. Preheat oven to 350°. In a large bowl, cream butter, shortening, brown sugar and salt until light and fluffy. Beat in egg yolk and vanilla. Gradually beat flour into creamed mixture. Refrigerate the dough, covered, until easy to handle, 30 minutes.

2. Preheat oven to 350°. Shape dough into 1¼-in. balls. In a shallow bowl, whisk egg white until foamy. Place almonds in a separate shallow bowl. Dip balls in egg white; roll in almonds.

3. Place 2 in. apart on ungreased baking sheets. Press a deep indentation in center of each with your thumb. Bake until the edges are light brown, 10-12 minutes. Remove from pans to wire racks.

4. In a small bowl, beat confectioners' sugar, cherry juice, butter and milk until smooth. Fill each cookie with ¼ tsp. filling; top with one cherry. Drizzle with candy coating. Let stand until set.

1 COOKIE: 145 cal., 9g fat (3g sat. fat), 14mg chol., 75mg sod., 15g carb. (10g sugars, 1g fiber), 2g pro.

GOOEY CHOCOLATE CARAMEL BARS

These rich, gooey bars are my most requested treats.
They're popular at school functions, family barbecues and picnics.
We like them alone or topped off with a scoop of ice cream.
—*Betty Hagerty, Philadelphia, PA*

PREP: 25 min. • **BAKE:** 20 min. + cooling • **MAKES:** about 4½ dozen

2¼ cups all-purpose flour, divided
2 cups quick-cooking oats
1½ cups packed brown sugar
1 tsp. baking soda
½ tsp. salt
1½ cups cold butter, cubed
2 cups (12 oz.) semisweet chocolate chips
1 cup chopped pecans
1 jar (12 oz.) caramel ice cream topping

1. In a large bowl, combine 2 cups flour, oats, brown sugar, baking soda and salt. Cut in butter until crumbly. Set half aside for topping.

2. Press the remaining crumb mixture into a greased 13x9-in. baking pan. Bake at 350° for 15 minutes. Sprinkle with the chocolate chips and pecans.

3. Whisk caramel topping and remaining flour until smooth; drizzle over top. Sprinkle with the reserved crumb mixture. Bake for 18-20 minutes or until golden brown. Cool on a wire rack for 2 hours before cutting.

1 BAR: 156 cal., 9g fat (5g sat. fat), 14mg chol., 110mg sod., 20g carb. (13g sugars, 1g fiber), 2g pro.

✳ READER RAVE

"I have made this numerous times. I make it for church functions, family gatherings, company and give them as gifts. Everyone who eats these bars loves them. They are super, super easy. This is one of my husband's favorite treats. He asks for them all the time. They freeze well, too."

—LUVROTTIES, TASTEOFHOME.COM

BLUEBERRY LATTICE BARS

Since our area has an annual blueberry festival, my daughters and I are always looking for great new berry recipes to enter in the cooking contest. These yummy bars won a blue ribbon one year.
—*Debbie Ayers, Baileyville, ME*

PREP: 25 min. + chilling • **BAKE:** 30 min. + cooling • **MAKES:** 2 dozen

1⅓ cups butter, softened
⅔ cup sugar
¼ tsp. salt
1 large egg
½ tsp. vanilla extract
3¾ cups all-purpose flour
FILLING
3 cups fresh or frozen blueberries
1 cup sugar
3 Tbsp. cornstarch

1. Cream butter, sugar and salt until light and fluffy; beat in egg and vanilla. Gradually beat in flour. Divide dough in half; shape each into a 1-in.-thick rectangle. Wrap in plastic; refrigerate 2 hours or overnight.

2. Preheat oven to 375°. Place blueberries, sugar and cornstarch in a small saucepan. Bring to a boil over medium heat, stirring frequently; cook and stir until thickened, about 2 minutes. Cool slightly.

3. Roll each portion of dough between two sheets of plastic wrap into a 14x10-in. rectangle. Place the rectangles on separate baking sheets; freeze until firm, 5-10 minutes. Place one dough rectangle in a greased 13x9-in. baking pan, pressing onto bottom and about ½ in. up the sides. Add filling.

4. Cut remaining rectangle into ½-in. strips; freeze 5-10 minutes to firm. Arrange strips over the filling in crisscross fashion. If desired, press edges with a fork to seal strips. Bake until the top crust is golden brown, 30-35 minutes. Cool on a wire rack. Cut into bars.

1 BAR: 233 cal., 11g fat (7g sat. fat), 35mg chol., 109mg sod., 32g carb. (16g sugars, 1g fiber), 3g pro.

BIG SOFT GINGER COOKIES

These nicely spiced, soft gingerbread cookies are perfect for folks who like the flavor of ginger but don't care for crunchy gingersnaps.
—*Barbara Gray, Boise, ID*

PREP: 20 min. • **BAKE:** 10 min./batch • **MAKES:** 2½ dozen

¾ cup butter, softened
1 cup sugar
1 large egg
¼ cup molasses
2¼ cups all-purpose flour
2 tsp. ground ginger
1 tsp. baking soda
¾ tsp. ground cinnamon
½ tsp. ground cloves
¼ tsp. salt
  Additional sugar

1. In a large bowl, cream butter and sugar until light and fluffy. Beat in egg and molasses. Combine the flour, ginger, baking soda, cinnamon, cloves and salt; gradually add to the creamed mixture and mix well.

2. Roll into 1½-in. balls, then roll in sugar. Place 2 in. apart on ungreased baking sheets. Bake at 350° until puffy and lightly browned, 10-12 minutes. Remove to wire racks to cool.

1 COOKIE: 111 cal., 5g fat (3g sat. fat), 19mg chol., 98mg sod., 16g carb. (8g sugars, 0 fiber), 1g pro.

✷ DID YOU KNOW?

Molasses is a byproduct of refining cane or beets into sugar. Light and dark molasses are made from the first and second cooking procedures, respectively. Blackstrap, made from the third procedure, is the strongest, darkest and most intensely flavored of the three. Dark molasses works well in most recipes.

TOFFEE ALMOND SANDIES

These crispy classics are loaded with crunchy chopped toffee and almonds, so there's no doubt as to why they're my husband's favorite cookie. I used to bake them in large batches when our four sons still lived at home. Now I make them for some very happy grandchildren.
—*Alice Kahnk, Kennard, NE*

PREP: 35 min. • **BAKE:** 15 min./batch • **MAKES:** about 12 dozen

1   cup butter, softened
1   cup sugar
1   cup confectioners' sugar
1   cup canola oil
2   large eggs
1   tsp. almond extract
3½ cups all-purpose flour
1   cup whole wheat flour
1   tsp. baking soda
1   tsp. cream of tartar
1   tsp. salt
2   cups chopped almonds
1   pkg. (8 oz.) milk chocolate English toffee bits
    Additional sugar

1. In a large bowl, cream butter and sugars until light and fluffy. Beat in the oil, eggs and extract. Combine flours, baking soda, cream of tartar and salt; gradually add to creamed mixture and mix well. Stir in almonds and toffee bits.

2. Shape into 1-in. balls; roll in sugar. Place balls on ungreased baking sheets and flatten with a fork. Bake at 350° until lightly browned, 12-14 minutes.

1 COOKIE: 68 cal., 4g fat (1g sat. fat), 7mg chol., 42mg sod., 6g carb. (3g sugars, 0 fiber), 1g pro.

OATMEAL CHOCOLATE CHIP PEANUT BUTTER BARS

Oatmeal, peanut butter and chocolate chips make these bars a hit with kids of all ages. Since I always have the ingredients on hand, I can whip up a batch anytime.
—*Patricia Staudt, Marble Rock, IA*

PREP: 15 min. • **BAKE:** 20 min. + cooling • **MAKES:** 4 dozen

½ cup butter, softened
½ cup sugar
½ cup packed brown sugar
½ cup creamy peanut butter
1 large egg
1 tsp. vanilla extract
1 cup all-purpose flour
½ cup quick-cooking oats
1 tsp. baking soda
¼ tsp. salt
1 cup (6 oz.) semisweet chocolate chips

ICING
½ cup confectioners' sugar
2 Tbsp. creamy peanut butter
2 Tbsp. milk

1. In a large bowl, cream the butter, sugars and peanut butter until light and fluffy. Beat in the egg and vanilla. Combine flour, oats, baking soda and salt; gradually beat into creamed mixture and mix well. Spread into a greased 13x9-in. baking pan. Sprinkle top of the bars with chocolate chips.

2. Bake at 350° for 20-25 minutes or until lightly browned. Cool on a wire rack for 10 minutes.

3. Combine icing ingredients; drizzle over the top. Cool completely. Cut into bars.

1 BAR: 90 cal., 5g fat (2g sat. fat), 9mg chol., 71mg sod., 11g carb. (8g sugars, 1g fiber), 1g pro.

✱ TEST KITCHEN TIP

Unless otherwise specified, *Taste of Home* recipes are tested with lightly salted butter. Unsalted, or sweet, butter is sometimes used to achieve a buttery flavor, such as in shortbread cookies or buttercream frosting. In those recipes, added salt would detract from the buttery taste desired.

FROSTED FUDGE BROWNIES

A neighbor brought over a pan of these rich brownies when I came home from the hospital with our baby daughter. I asked her how to make brownies like that, and I've made them ever since for all sorts of occasions. They're great!

—*Sue Soderlund, Elgin, IL*

PREP: 10 min. + cooling • **BAKE:** 25 min. + cooling • **MAKES:** 2 dozen

1 cup plus 3 Tbsp. butter, cubed
¾ cup baking cocoa
4 large eggs
2 cups sugar
1½ cups all-purpose flour
1 tsp. baking powder
1 tsp. salt
1 tsp. vanilla extract

FROSTING
6 Tbsp. butter, softened
2⅔ cups confectioners' sugar
½ cup baking cocoa
1 tsp. vanilla extract
¼ to ⅓ cup whole milk

1. In a saucepan, melt butter. Remove from the heat. Stir in cocoa; cool. In a large bowl, beat eggs and sugar until blended. Combine flour, baking powder and salt; gradually add to egg mixture. Stir in vanilla and the cooled chocolate mixture until well blended.

2. Spread into a greased 13x9-in. baking pan. Bake at 350° for 25-28 minutes or until a toothpick inserted in the center comes out clean (do not overbake). Cool on a wire rack.

3. For frosting, in a large bowl, cream the butter and confectioners' sugar until light and fluffy. Beat in the cocoa and vanilla. Add enough milk until the frosting achieves spreading consistency. Spread over brownies. Cut into bars.

1 SERVING: 277 cal., 13g fat (8g sat. fat), 68mg chol., 248mg sod., 39g carb. (29g sugars, 1g fiber), 3g pro.

RECIPE INDEX